PRACTICING GRAMMAR AND USAGE

Revised by:

Carlos Hernandez
The City University of New York

PRENTICE HALL
REFERENCE GUIDE

SEVENTH EDITION

Muriel Harris
Purdue University

PEARSON
Prentice
Hall

Upper Saddle River, New Jersey 07458

© 2008 by PEARSON EDUCATION, INC.
Upper Saddle River, New Jersey 07458

10 9 8 7 6 5 4 3 2 1

ISBN 10: 0-13-237954-6
ISBN 13: 978-0-13-237954-0

Printed in the United States of America

CONTENTS

Part Seven: Punctuation

Part Eight: Mechanics and Spelling

Part Nine: ESL and Multilingual Writers

Part Ten: Research

Part Eleven: MLA Documentation

Part Twelve: APA, CM, and CSE Documentation

Answer Key

PART TWO
THE WRITING PROCESS

Chapter 1 Thinking About Writing

1a. The Rhetorical Triangle

Situation: Alan has written an excellent paper on the problem of child obesity in the U.S., and his professor has asked him to present it at a symposium that the college is sponsoring. Alan's thesis is that the government should play an active role in combating the child obesity -- even if tax increases were necessary to fund its initiatives.

The professor has asked Alan to tailor his essay to the symposium. To do that, Alan will need to keep the parts of the rhetorical triangle in mind:

Topic: What facts on the topic are undisputed? What do leading experts say about the topic? What are the various sides of the issue, and what groups support them?

Writer: What do I believe about the subject? What evidence do I have to support my beliefs? Do I feel that there is more than one right answer to this issue?

Audience: What does my audience believe about the subject? Are my beliefs in conflict with the audience's? Is the audience heterogeneous (that is, is it made up of people with differing beliefs)? How do I think they will react to my ideas?

Context: Is there anything happening in the world that might influence how people will react to my topic? Does my topic have political implications? Will the timing or location have an impact on my message?

Assignment: For each of the conditions below, describe some of the factors Alan might need to consider to tailor his paper for the symposium.

1. The audience for the symposium will be made up primarily of concerned parents.

_____

_____

_____

_____

_____

2. A new scientific study has found that fourth graders who bring their lunches to school are less likely to be obese than fourth graders who buy their lunches at school.

_____

_____

_____

_____

_____

3. Breaking news! A popular reality TV show in which overweight children go to summer camp to lose weight is being investigated for possible child endangerment.

_____

_____

_____

_____

_____

4. Alan's professor has also invited the campus's Young Republican club to the symposium to provide a different opinion on Alan's ideas about raising taxes and creating a larger government to combat child obesity.

_____

_____

_____

_____

_____

lb. Topic

In order to find a topic for a piece of writing, assume that an interviewer or reporter is asking you the following questions, and write your responses to those questions. An example of a possible answer to the first question is given here.

EXAMPLE

What is a problem you'd like to solve?

> Businesses downtown have a problem attracting customers since there is nowhere to park; a parking garage might help revitalize the city.

1. What is a problem you'd like to solve?

_____

_____

_____

_____

2. What is something that pleases, puzzles, irritates, or bothers you?

_____

_____

_____

_____

3. What is something you'd like to convince others of?

_____

_____

_____

_____

4. What is something that seems to contradict what you read or see around you?

_____

_____

_____

_____

5. What is something you'd like to learn more about?

_____

_____

_____

_____

6. What is something you know about that others around you may not know?

_____

_____

_____

_____

1c. Audience

In order to be sure that the information you write is helpful to your readers, consider more fully and carefully the general audience you targeted for the topics in the previous exercise. Analyze each audience by answering the questions below.

1. Topic: **television**   Target audience: _____

    a. What do the readers already know about the topic, and what new information will they need?

_____

_____

_____

_____

_____

    b. What is the audience's attitude toward the subject?

_____

_____

_____

_____

_____

    c. What is the audience's background?

_____

_____

_____

_____

_____

d. What tone or level of formality should you use?

_____

_____

_____

_____

_____

2. **Topic:** human cloning   Target audience: _____

   a. What do the readers already know about the topic, and what new information will they need?

_____

_____

_____

_____

_____

   b. What is the audience's attitude toward the subject?

_____

_____

_____

_____

   c. What is the audience's background?

_____

_____

_____

_____

d.   What tone or level of formality should you use?

_____

_____

_____

_____

_____

3.   **Topic:** sports   Target audience: _____

a.   What do the readers already know about the topic, and what new information will they need?

_____

_____

_____

_____

_____

b.   What is the audience's attitude toward the subject?

_____

_____

_____

_____

_____

c.   What is the audience's background?

_____

_____

_____

_____

_____

d.   What tone or level of formality should you use?

_____

_____

_____

_____

_____

1d. Purpose

For each of the purposes for writing listed below, create a situation in which you might write with that purpose in mind. An example of a situation for the first purpose, "Summarizing," is given here.

EXAMPLE

Summarizing:

> I work for a consumer finance company, and my job is to look over an applicant's credit history: credit report, information from the application, etc. I must summarize the credit history in a single paragraph for the loan officer who will make the final decision.

1.   Summarizing:

_____

_____

_____

_____

2.   Defining:

_____

_____

_____

_____

3. Analyzing:

_____

_____

_____

_____

4. Persuading:

_____

_____

_____

_____

5. Reporting:

_____

_____

_____

_____

6. Evaluating:

_____

_____

_____

_____

7. Discussing/Examining:

_____

_____

_____

_____

8. Interpreting:

_____

_____

_____

_____

1e. Medium

Situation: The New York State Department of Health has hired your advertising agency to help it conduct its "Eliminating Childhood Lead Poisoning in New York State by 2010" campaign. Specifically, they want you to produce three things:

1. An arresting poster that can be placed on New York City subways and in government agencies around the State that communicates to the public the need for awareness about the dangers lead poses to children.

The poster should contain the following elements:
- An image that will stop people in their tracks and capture their interest.
- A single phrase or sentence in large font at the top of the advertisement that will further hook viewers.
- A very brief (2-3 sentence) explanation of childhood lead poisoning, near the bottom of the poster.
- The web site where people can get more information: http://www.health.state.ny.us/environmental/lead/index.htm .

Use the space provided below to design your poster.

2. A design for a web site that will provide information about the dangers of lead and what parents, landlords, and communities can do to combat the problem. The web site should contain the following elements:
- An interesting banner for the New York State Department of Health's site on eliminating childhood lead poisoning.
- A list of links that will help users navigate the web site. You will need to anticipate what types of information visitors to the site will want to find. Then, create a list of appropriate links to help them find what they need to know.
- An introductory welcome statement explaining the purpose of the site, the information that can be found on the site, and, for those unfamiliar with web pages, how to navigate it.

Draw banner below.

Write site navigation links above.

Write welcome message above.

3. A short, formal letter that will go to New York State legislators, urging them to help combat childhood lead poisoning in their districts.

_____

_____

_____

_____

_____

_____

_____

_____

_____

_____

_____

_____

_____

_____

1f. Thesis

Narrow each of the following topics by asking yourself the series of questions listed with each topic. Then write the thesis that has developed from your answers. Analyze your thesis by underlining your topic once and your comment about it twice. An example is given here.

EXAMPLE

Topic: Carpentry

Who am I in this piece of writing?	I am someone with knowledge to share.
Who is my intended audience?	Readers of a do-it-yourself newsletter.
What is the purpose of this writing?	To inform.
What are some other conditions that will shape this writing?	Length (space provided in the newsletter for this article), format, demographics of the audience (age, basic level of knowledge of carpentry).

Thesis:

Building an attractive and efficient computer desk can be an easy and affordable weekend project.

_____

1. Topic: Television

Who am I in this piece of writing? _____

Who is my intended audience? _____

What is the purpose of this writing _____

What are some other conditions that will shape this writing? _____

_____

_____

Thesis: _____

_____

_____

2. Topic: Human cloning

Who am I in this piece of writing? _____

Who is my intended audience? _____

What is the purpose of this writing? _____

What are some other conditions that will shape this writing? _____

_____

_____

Thesis: _____

_____

_____

3. **Topic: Sports**

Who am I in this piece of writing? _____

Who is my intended audience? _____

What is the purpose of this writing? _____

What are some other conditions that will shape this writing? _____

_____

_____

Thesis: _____

_____

_____

Chapter 2 Writing Processes and Strategies

2a. Planning

Use the planning strategies listed below to find material you might want to include in writing about the corresponding topics. An example of one planning strategy, "Brainstorming," is given here.

EXAMPLE

Topic: Choosing a college

Planning Strategy: Brainstorming

deciding between a state university and a private college
reasons to go to a state university
- close to home
- in-state tuition much less than private college
- large selection of classes
- popular sports teams
- research facilities

reasons to go to a private college
- smaller classes
- prestige
- less chance of being lost in the crowd
- even freshmen always taught by professors

checking out college flyers
checking out magazine articles on colleges
visiting college campuses
talking to friends and family who have attended college
knowing how much I can afford and not going above it
grades/acceptance
what SAT/ACT scores are required choosing a roommate

1. Topic: Paying for college

   Planning Strategy: Brainstorming

   _____

   _____

   _____

2.   Topic: Comparing American dating to dating in another culture

Planning Strategy: Freewriting

_____

_____

_____

_____

3.   Topic: Rock music

Planning Strategy: Listing

_____

_____

_____

_____

4.   Topic: Violence on television

Planning Strategy: Clustering and Branching

_____

_____

_____

_____

5.   Topic: How to choose a college

Planning Strategy: Outlining

_____

_____

_____

_____

6. Topic: Drinking and driving

   Planning Strategy: Who?—what?—when?—where?—how?—why?

   _____

   _____

   _____

   _____

2b–2c. Drafting and Organizing

Using one of the topics and planning strategies you completed in 2a, draft and organize a paper on that topic.

_____

_____

_____

_____

_____

_____

_____

_____

_____

_____

_____

_____

_____

_____

2d. Collaborating

Using one of the following methods, get responses from readers of the draft of the paper you completed in 2b-2c: meeting with a writing-center tutor, meeting with a small group of students in your class, or meeting with a writing group you form on your own. Ask your readers to respond to the questions below about your paper, and record their responses to each question.

1. What do the readers like about this draft?

   _____

   _____

2. What do the readers think is the main point of this paper?

   _____

   _____

3. Are there any sections that are unclear and need more explanation?

   _____

   _____

4. Does the paper fit the assignment?

   _____

   _____

5. Who is the appropriate reader or audience for the paper?

   _____

   _____

6. Are there any sections of the paper that seem out of order?

   _____

   _____

7. Are there any sections of the paper where the writing seems to digress from the topic?

   _____

   _____

8. Does the paper flow?

_____

_____

9. What else do your readers want to know about the paper's topic?

_____

_____

10. What is the most important revision to your paper your readers would suggest?

_____

_____

2e. Revising

Using the responses you gathered in 2d above and the revision checklist of higher-order concerns (HOCs), revise your paper for greater effectiveness.

_____

_____

_____

_____

_____

_____

_____

_____

_____

_____

2f. Editing and Proofreading

Using the checklist of later-order concerns (LOCs), edit your paper for details of grammar, usage, punctuation, spelling, and other mechanics. After editing for LOCs, proofread your paper one last time for missing words, misspellings, and format. Then write the final draft of your paper below.

_____

_____

_____

_____

_____

_____

_____

_____

_____

_____

_____

_____

_____

_____

_____

_____

_____

Chapter 3 Paragraphs

3a. Unity

Read the sample paragraph below, and then write a short paragraph describing what aspects of unity are present or missing.

A recent expedition to Tibet resulted in the discovery of a previously unknown species of a small horse. The horses are only about four feet tall, but they are very strong. Expedition members experienced a great deal of bad weather during their stay in Tibet. Even though the discovery of the tiny horses caused much excitement in the scientific world, the local citizens seem to take them for granted and use them as pack animals.

_____

_____

_____

_____

_____

_____

_____

_____

_____

_____

_____

_____

_____

_____

3b. Coherence

Read the sample paragraph below, and then write a short paragraph describing what aspects of coherence are present or missing.

> Although many people think of the interior of Alaska as flat expanses of ice and snow, the geography of the area is actually quite varied. The interior of Alaska has long, cold winters and mild, short summers. The climate is actually quite dry, but most of the precipitation that does fall is in the winter and is in the form of snow. Twenty-three languages are spoken in the interior of Alaska. The area was home to forest dwelling bands of natives in historic times.

_____

_____

_____

_____

_____

_____

_____

_____

_____

_____

3c. Development

Read the sample paragraph below, and then write a short paragraph describing whether its development is adequate or inadequate and why.

> Blade II is a really good movie. It stars Wesley Snipes and is about vampires. It is really exciting and is a sequel to the first movie–Blade.

_____

_____

_____

_____

_____

_____

_____

_____

_____

_____

3d. Introductions and Conclusions

1. Ask several classmates how they go about writing an introductory paragraph for a longer piece of writing. Write a short paragraph describing the different ways people draft an introductory paragraph.

_____

_____

_____

_____

_____

_____

_____

_____

2. Ask several classmates how they go about writing a concluding paragraph for a longer piece of writing. Write a short paragraph describing the different ways people draft a conclusion.

_____

_____

_____

_____

_____

_____

_____

_____

_____

_____

3c. Patterns of Organization

For each of the patterns of organization listed below, write a paragraph using that pattern on the topic provided.

1. Pattern of Organization: Narration

    Topic: An experience that taught you a valuable lesson

_____

_____

_____

_____

_____

_____

_____

_____

_____

_____

_____

_____

_____

2. Pattern of Organization: Description

   Topic: A place where you go to think

   _____

   _____

   _____

   _____

   _____

   _____

   _____

   _____

   _____

3. Pattern of Organization: Cause and Effect

   Topic: Why you chose your current major/course schedule

   _____

   _____

   _____

   _____

   _____

   _____

   _____

   _____

   _____

   _____

4. Pattern of Organization: Analogy

   Topic: The impact of the Internet on American society

   _____

   _____

   _____

   _____

   _____

   _____

   _____

   _____

5. Pattern of Organization: Example

   Topic: Contemporary heroes

   _____

   _____

   _____

   _____

   _____

   _____

   _____

   _____

   _____

6. Pattern of Organization: Illustration

    Topic: "Reality" television shows

    _____

    _____

    _____

    _____

    _____

    _____

    _____

    _____

    _____

7. Pattern of Organization: Classification

    Topic: Contemporary music

    _____

    _____

    _____

    _____

    _____

    _____

    _____

    _____

    _____

8. Pattern of Organization: Division

   Topic: College life

   _____

   _____

   _____

   _____

   _____

   _____

   _____

   _____

   _____

9. Pattern of Organization: Process Analysis

   Topic: Finding a job

   _____

   _____

   _____

   _____

   _____

   _____

   _____

   _____

   _____

10. Pattern of Organization: Compare and contrast

Topic: Two places you have visited

_____

_____

_____

_____

_____

_____

_____

_____

_____

11. Pattern of Organization: Definition

Topic: Success

_____

_____

_____

_____

_____

_____

_____

_____

Chapter 4 Argument

4a-4c. Writing and Reading Arguments, Considering the Audience, and Finding a Topic

Choose a topic for a persuasive paper which is arguable, interesting, or of local concern. Once you have chosen your topic, decide on the appropriate audience for your topic, your purpose for the argument, the kinds of appeals you will use to make your case, and the common ground you share with your audience. If you have difficulty coming up with a topic of your own, you may choose from one of the following: smoking laws; the role of the United States as a world peacekeeper; the use of personality tests as a requirement for employment; a particular investment method as opposed to others (for example, investing in mutual funds as opposed to the stock market); or a local bond issue.

Topic _____

Audience _____

Purpose _____

Appeals _____

_____

Common Ground _____

_____

4d. Developing Your Arguments

1. Using the same topic for writing and the ideas you began planning in the last exercise, begin developing your argument by clarifying what your main point or claim is, what support you will offer for that claim, what warrants or unspoken assumptions are present in the argument, and what form of development (inductive or deductive) will be most effective.

Your claim _____

_____

The type of support you will use to convince the audience _____

_____

Warrants in the argument _____

_____

Method of development (inductive or deductive) _____

2. Consider how to avoid errors in reasoning in your argument by writing examples of logical fallacies about your topic which you would NOT use in a persuasive paper. By recognizing what you will not use as an argument, you will be better prepared to decide what you will use.

a. Hasty Generalization

_____

_____

b. Begging the Question (circular reasoning)

_____

_____

c. Doubtful Cause (post hoc, ergo propter hoc)

_____

_____

d. Using Irrelevant Proof to Support a Claim (non-sequitur)

_____

_____

e. False Analogy

_____

_____

f. Attack the Person (ad hominem)

_____

_____

g. Either ...Or

_____

_____

h. Bandwagon

_____

_____

3. For more practice in logic, use the list above to identify the logical fallacies in the following statements or arguments. Write a label that names the fallacy; then explain how the example illustrates that fallacy.

a. A vote for the President is a vote for our troops who are in harm's way; a vote for his opponent shows a lack of support for our troops.

Fallacy _____

Explanation _____

_____

b. This candidate had a reported income of over 6 million dollars last year. How can he possibly understand and help all the people in this country who don't have enough money to feed their children?

Fallacy _____

Explanation _____

_____

c. I'm going to vote for this candidate because everyone who cares about the values I care about is voting for him.

Fallacy _____

Explanation _____

_____

d. Assisted suicide, even though based on the desires of the person involved, should be illegal because anyone who wants to commit suicide is obviously incompetent and not capable of making rational decisions.

Fallacy _____

Explanation _____

_____

e.   This candidate will not defend the country against attacks by our enemies. Throughout his career in Congress he has consistently voted against military spending.

Fallacy _____

Explanation _____

_____

4e. Recognizing and Avoiding Fallacies

For each of the numbered sentences below, write what type of fallacy it is using as (faulty) evidence to support its claims. You may choose from "Hasty Generalization," "Begging the Question," "Doubtful Cause," "Irrelevant Proof," "False Analogy," "Personal Attack," "Either ... Or," or "Bandwagon." If a sentence, does not commit a logical fallacy, write "No fallacy" for that sentence.

1. I've never met a person who didn't want lower taxes, so how can all of those people be wrong?

2. Lower taxes would lead to a higher quality of life for everyone.

3. We have a choice: either lower taxes or weaken the economy.

4. If we can send a man to the moon, we should be able to run our government without taxing our people so heavily.

5. Some congressional leaders say high taxes are necessary, but that's because they're so rich they can afford to pay them -- or hire sleazy accountants who find tax loopholes for them.

6. According to lassie faire economics, lowering taxes might encourage spending, which in turn may help shorten the duration of an economic recession.

7. The government makes so many mistakes because we give it so much money; if we cut taxes, it would have less money and would therefore commit fewer errors.

8. In 2000, the government announced it would issue tax refund checks to most lower- and middle-income Americans. In that same year, the crime rate in the U.S. dropped to its lowest rate since 1966. This proves that charging less for taxes lowers crime.

9. It's the government's job to benefit its people, and everyone would benefit from lower taxes.

10. We know the tax code is messed up because the government created it. Everything the government creates is messed up. If you don't believe me, just look at the tax code.

4f. Organizing Your Arguments

Decide upon the most effective organization for the argument you were developing above and justify why you have chosen that pattern of organization.

Pattern of Organization _____

Justification _____

_____

_____

(Now that you have completed Exercises 4a-4e, you should be prepared to draft, revise, and edit a persuasive paper on your topic if your instructor requires it.)

Chapter 5 Visual Argument

Develop a visual argument for each of the situations described below.   Remember to consider these questions as you plan each visual argument:

- What claim do you want to make? (i.e., what is your point or thesis?)
- Who is the audience and what beliefs can you assume they have?
- What shared images can you draw on that will be immediately recognizable to the audience?
- How can you make connections between the claim and the images?
- Which images will have an emotional impact without overpowering the logic of the argument?
- Do you need a speaker to contribute ethical appeal?
- Is the image sufficient to be effective, or do you need carefully chosen words to enhance it?
- Are you avoiding obvious logical fallacies?

In the spaces below, describe (and draw if you wish) the image you would use.

1.   As a teaching intern at a middle school, you are asked to develop an image to persuade students not to begin (or to stop) smoking.

_____

_____

_____

_____

_____

_____

_____

_____

2.   As an active student member of the Republican or Democratic party, develop a visual argument to persuade successful, college-educated twenty-something professionals who have never voted to do so in the current election.

_____

_____

_____

_____

_____

_____

_____

_____

_____

_____

3. As an activist in your suburban neighborhood, develop a visual argument to persuade your neighbors to have their pets neutered.

_____

_____

_____

_____

_____

_____

_____

_____

_____

Chapter 6 Document Design

6a. Principles of Document Design

Group the information in the paragraph below into a list that will be less crowded and have more white space.

The restaurant guide has lists of ethnic restaurants. They list Chinese restaurants in the city. They also list Italian restaurants and Mexican restaurants. As an extra feature, they list ethnic restaurants by neighborhood.

_____

_____

_____

_____

_____

_____

_____

_____

6b. Incorporating Visuals

1. Put the information in the paragraph below into a **bar graph** to add interest to your Web page.

    College freshmen at the university took an average of 18 credit hours per semester. Sophomores took an average of 16 hours per semester and juniors and seniors took an average of 12 hours per semester.

2. Now put the same information in a **line graph**.

3. List all the activities that you participate in during a typical weekday, say a Tuesday, during this semester. Determine the number of hours you spend in each activity, and construct a **pie chart** that displays the information.

6c. Paper Preparation

Identify each of the pages below as belonging in MLA or APA style.

1. Title Page　　　　　　　　　　　　　　　　＿＿＿＿＿＿＿＿＿＿＿＿＿

2. First page, with author information　　　　　＿＿＿＿＿＿＿＿＿＿＿＿＿

3. Tables (on a separate page)　　　　　　　　＿＿＿＿＿＿＿＿＿＿＿＿＿

4. Footnotes　　　　　　　　　　　　　　　　＿＿＿＿＿＿＿＿＿＿＿＿＿

5. Works Cited List　　　　　　　　　　　　　＿＿＿＿＿＿＿＿＿＿＿＿＿

6. Appendixes　　　　　　　　　　　　　　　＿＿＿＿＿＿＿＿＿＿＿＿＿

7. End notes　　　　　　　　　　　　　　　　＿＿＿＿＿＿＿＿＿＿＿＿＿

6d. Multimedia Presentations

As The Prentice Hall Reference Guide notes, a hilarious and telling satire on PowerPoint presentations can be found at http://norvig.com/Gettysburg/ . But we should not conclude from that example that all multimedia presentations are destined to similar kinds of shallow buffoonery. The key is to suit the use of media to the occasion.

Below is the full text of the Gettysburg address (taken from "Abraham Lincoln Online." http://showcase.netins.net/web/creative/lincoln/speeches/gettysburg.htm . 9/23/07. 9/24/07.)

Read the text, then, either alone or with a group, outline a plan for a multimedia presentation for the 150th anniversary of the Gettysburg Address (which will happen in 2013). The presentation must communicate to modern viewers both the solemnity of the original occasion that prompted the speech and the monumental importance of the speech to American history.

"Four score and seven years ago our fathers brought forth on this continent, a new nation, conceived in Liberty, and dedicated to the proposition that all men are created equal.

"Now we are engaged in a great civil war, testing whether that nation, or any nation so conceived and so dedicated, can long endure. We are met on a great battle-field of that war. We have come to dedicate a portion of that field, as a final resting place for those who here gave their lives that that nation might live. It is altogether fitting and proper that we should do this.

"But, in a larger sense, we can not dedicate -- we can not consecrate -- we can not hallow -- this ground. The brave men, living and dead, who struggled here, have consecrated it, far above our poor power to add or detract. The world will little note, nor long remember what we say here, but it can never forget what they did here. It is for us the living, rather, to be dedicated here to the unfinished work which they who fought here have thus far so nobly advanced. It is rather for us to be here dedicated to the great task remaining before us -- that from these honored dead we take increased devotion to that cause for which they gave the last full measure of devotion -- that we here highly resolve that these dead shall not have died in vain -- that this nation, under God, shall have a new birth of freedom -- and that government of the people, by the people, for the people, shall not perish from the earth."

6e. Web Page Design

1. Draw a visual plan for a webpage for an online clothing store that would include the following pages:

   - Home Page

   - Men's clothing

   - Women's clothing

   - Children's clothing

   - Dresses

   - Toddlers

   - Children's sizes 5-10

2. If you do not already have a personal website, follow the steps below to begin planning your website.

   a. Describe the purpose for your website (e.g., entertainment, persuasion, seeking employment).

   _____

   _____

   _____

   _____

   b. Describe your home page and/or draw a replica of it here:

c. Draw a visual plan for your website, showing all the pages that will link to your homepage. Include as many levels of pages as you anticipate producing.

PART THREE
COMMON CATEGORIES OF WRITING

Chapter 7 Writing About Literature

7a. Ways to Write About Literature

Read a play or short story. Briefly describe each of the following aspects of the work:

1. **Plot**—How do events connect? Do some events foreshadow others?

_____

_____

_____

_____

_____

_____

_____

_____

_____

_____

2. **Characters**—Who is the main character in the work? Does this character change and if so, how?

_____

_____

_____

_____

_____

_____

_____

_____

_____

_____

_____

3. **Narrative Structure**—Do the events proceed in chronological order? What clues does the author provide?

_____

_____

_____

_____

_____

_____

_____

_____

_____

_____

4. **Narrator**—Is a character telling the story? If so, how does this affect how we see the action? If not, how much are we shown (thoughts, movement in place, time, etc.)?

_____

_____

_____

_____

_____

_____

_____

_____

_____

5. **Gender**—How does the work portray men and women? Is there a difference in how each is portrayed?

_____

_____

_____

_____

_____

_____

_____

_____

_____

_____

6. **Genre**—How would you describe the type of literature this work represents (give specific reasons for your choice)?

_____

_____

_____

_____

_____

_____

_____

_____

_____

_____

7c. Conventions in Writing About Literature

Next to each example below, identify the verb tense that should be used.

1. A biography of the author _____

2. A brief summary of a short story _____

3. Introducing a line from a poem _____

4. Describing the environment in which a novel was written _____

Chapter 8 Professional Writing

8a.-8b. Memos and E-Mail Communications

Write a memo or an e-mail about a situation or a problem that has arisen in the student club of which you are president. Explain the situation and propose a solution. The correspondence should be addressed to the sponsor of the club. You may write the correspondence here or type and print it.

_____

_____

_____

_____

_____

_____

_____

_____

_____

_____

_____

_____

_____

_____

_____

_____

_____

_____

8c. Business Letters

Write a letter recommending a person for employment. The body of your text should contain at least two paragraphs. The person to whom you are writing is Phil Brannan, New Projects Director. The address is 128 Cedar Ave., Overland Park, Kansas 66212. Be sure to send a copy to Monica Oden, Director of Human Resources. This letter should be typed or word processed and printed.

_____

_____

_____

_____

_____

_____

_____

_____

_____

_____

_____

_____

_____

_____

_____

_____

_____

8d. Cover Letters

Rewrite the letter below to make it an appropriate cover letter for a job.

222 Lanbow Road
Seabrook, NH 03874
may 13

Mr. Donald Wasserman
LPIN Financial
224 Eden Avenue, Suite 7S
Washington, DC 20055

Dear Mr. Wasserman

Hi! We met at a job fair at my school a few months ago, and at that time you told me there would be a job coming open in June. I want to get the entry-level position in the accounting department, which makes sense, since I graduate with a 3.9 GPA in my major, which was Accounting. I have also had two internships, one with Tunrow and Gaddis and the other with a firm you probably never heard of, but they were great there and I had a great experience. So why should you hire me? Because I am competent, a hard worker, responsible, a team-players, smart, committed, and work well with others. I also have the experience you need. Like I said above, I've had two internships that have helped me grow both personally and professionally. I also was Treasurer of our Accounting Club for three years, Treasuer of our Phi Beta Kappa chapter, and a Math and Accounting Tutoring in our Tutoring Center. My hobbies include snowboarding and crossword puzzles.

I know you have a lot of candidates applying for this job, but I hope you will give me an interview. Let me know either way.

Sincerely,

George Logan

Enclosure: Resume

8e. Résumés

1. Take the following Skills Resume and reorganize it into a Reverse Chronological Resume. The revised resume should be typed or word processed and printed out.

Donald Bryant

3256 Winslow Lane
Springfield, MO 65802
(417) 555-5300
dbryant@dotcom.net

PROFESSIONAL OBJECTIVE
A career in hotel management that would involve guest relations, scheduling and vendor management.

EDUCATION
Johnson County Community College
Associate in Applied Science Degree in Hotel/Motel Management
GPA (4.0 scale): 3.6
Major-Related Courses:
HOSPITALITY MANAGEMENT FUNDAMENTALS, FOOD MANAGEMENT, SUPERVISORY MANAGEMENT, HOSPITALITY LAW, SEMINAR IN HOUSEKEEPING OPERATIONS, HOTEL SALES AND MARKETING, ADVANCED HOSPITALITY MANAGEMENT, FRONT OFFICE MANAGEMENT, HOTEL ACCOUNTING

SKILLS
Accounting
- Student Senate Treasurer
- Did bookkeeping for local hobby store

Scheduling
- Events coordinator for Student Senate
- Scheduled work hours for College book store employees

Vendor relations
- Worked with various food vendors at mall food court

WORK EXPERIENCE
Assistant Manager, Oak Park Mall Food Court; August 2001 to present Assistant Manager, College Bookstore; Fall 2000-Spring 2001

2. Type a cover letter to accompany the revised resume.

PART FOUR
REVISING SENTENCES

Chapter 10 Comma Splices and Fused Sentences

The following paragraph contains some sentences that are punctuated incorrectly, some comma splices, and some fused sentences. Correct all the punctuation errors.

Our country seems to be going through a change in attitudes. Unlike our forefathers, we Americans are now encouraged to get as much as possible as quickly as possible. This attitude is expressed on television advertising also plays on this appeal. Many see a relationship between these current attitudes and gambling on lotteries, it is easy to understand why more and more people are handing their money over to chance, fate and luck if what they are looking for is instant gratification. Statistics show this attitude is growing, in the late 80s, state lotteries grew an average of 17.5 percent annually—roughly as fast as the computer industry. High-tech advertising for the lotteries takes attention away from the fact that a player has virtually no chance of winning, advertisements focus instead on the fantasy of what it would be like to win. Surveys conducted by state lotteries show that few players have a clear understanding of how dismal their odds of winning really are, a player has a better chance of being struck by lightning than of winning a lottery.

Chapter 11 Subject-Verb Agreement

1. In the following paragraph, underline the verb that agrees with the subject.

      A business that is growing rapidly in popularity as well as in profits (is, are) selling meteorites to collectors, museums, universities, and research laboratories. The usual meteorite that dealers offer to customers (weigh, weighs) only a few grams or less, but sometimes, someone out collecting meteorites (find, finds) a piece that can weigh over 100 pounds. Either a whole large meteorite or some chunks (sells, sell) for thousands of dollars. But in some countries the government (is, are) beginning to pass laws that forbid the export of meteorites. None of these governments (want, wants) these national treasures to leave their countries. The price for meteorites (depend, depends) on the rarity of that kind. How much is known to exist (is, are) an important factor in determining the rarity of any specimen that is found. Of the three classes of meteorites, "irons"—made up of iron and nickel—are common, though they represent less than 10 percent of all meteorites that (strike, strikes) the Earth. But they survive the intense heat of entering the atmosphere better than other meteorites (does, do) and can be easily found with a metal detector. All other meteorites, which (is, are) made of stone, are the most common ones that are found. Among these there (is, are) some that may have come from nearby planets when meteorites hit their surfaces. Having a piece of Mars (is, are) a good way to start a collection.

2. As you complete the following sentences, make sure the verb agrees with the subject. For this exercise, use only present or past tense verbs. For example, you could write I am happy, or I was happy, but do not write I will be happy.

a. I _____

    _____

b. We _____

    _____

c. Nearly all of my sister's clothes which she wears to school _____

    _____

d. The store clerks and their manager _____

_____

e. Either Carlos or his brothers _____

_____

f. Not only the players but also the coach _____

_____

g What I want to explain _____

_____

h To feel successful _____

_____

i. Each _____

_____

j Some of the examples _____

_____

k. Some of the assignment _____

_____

l. The committee _____

_____

m. Cryogenics _____

_____

n. The scissors _____

_____

o. Acme Enterprises _____

_____

p. Her idea (complete this sentence using a linking verb) _____

_____

q. Magazine articles (complete this sentence using a linking verb) _____

_____

r. There _____ an interesting book on the history of television in the library.

s. There _____ many books on the history of television in the library.

t. It _____ his beliefs that formed the basis for his argument.

u. They are the people who _____

_____

v. She is the person who _____

_____

w. Mr. Baker is one of those instructors who _____

_____

Chapter 12 Sentence Fragments

1. The following paragraph has both fragments and complete sentences. Identify each sentence as either a fragment or a complete sentence.

(1) A fierce battle has developed in American schools over the question of using English in the classroom. (2) Historically, immigrants coming to America were expected to learn English and to be taught in English. (3) Though that did not mean that they had to reject their original culture or language. (4) But for many, using English in school meant that their ethnic legacy would no longer dominate. (5) That it would disappear as they became fluent English speakers. (6) As a result, the emphasis on English as the dominant language was seen by many as discriminatory. (7) While others see this emphasis as the only way to have a common American culture that all children can share. (8) One answer to this has been bilingual education in which children who speak another language are taught academic subjects in their native language. (9) This transitional program which helps them to move along through school while they acquire English. (10) Bilingual education being the answer for some who want to preserve children's culture and provide schooling for them as they learn English. (11) Although others see it as a failed system because it segregates limited-English children into separate classrooms and dooms them to unskilled jobs where competence in English is less important. (12) They point out that children need to learn English in order to get better jobs, go on to college, and become full members of American society

1. _____

2. _____

3. _____

4. _____

5. _____

6. _____

7. _____

8. _____

9. _____

10. _____

11. _____

12. _____

2. Revise the sentences you identified above as fragments so that they are complete sentences. Write the number from the list above; then rewrite the sentence.

_____

_____

_____

_____

_____

_____

_____

_____

_____

_____

_____

_____

_____

_____

_____

_____

Chapter 13 Dangling and Misplaced Modifiers

13a.   Dangling Modifiers

1.   Underline the dangling modifiers in the following paragraph.

The great memorials in the nation's capital are slowly deteriorating. Having faced the elements for seven decades, even casual tourists can see that the Lincoln Memorial is wearing down. Water is causing the steel structures embedded in the concrete slabs to deteriorate. At the Jefferson Memorial, which is built on clay fill, the steps are starting to pull away from the base of the monument, and there are cracks appearing in the dome. Being washed daily, details in the marble carvings of both monuments are falling off. Air pollution and acid rain are also contributing to the gradual disintegration. To find a solution, constant studies by the National Park Service are being conducted, but the caretakers of the monuments are pessimistic. Exposure to the elements, they say, causes some deterioration that cannot be stopped. Looking more like ruins than buildings, it is hard to watch these noble monuments wear away.

2.   Rewrite the sentences with dangling modifiers that you identified in the exercise above, eliminating the modifier errors.

_____

_____

_____

_____

_____

_____

_____

_____

_____

_____

_____

13b. Misplaced Modifiers

1. In the following paragraph, underline the misplaced modifiers.

    The Food and Drug Administration (FDA) claims that it has found tiny amounts of drug residue in milk samples in a report issued recently. The level of contamination is so low that there is no real safety problem in the nation's milk supply, but a ban has been put on one drug, sulfamethazine, found in a few samples, to prohibit its use with beef cattle and pigs by farmers. The FDA has already banned the use of sulfamethazine with milk cows. However, there is still concern that some dairy farmers or veterinarians use the drug improperly among members of Congress, even though recent testing of milk samples only found a few traces of sulfa drugs in a large number. The FDA is now calling on dairy farmers and veterinarians to eliminate all illegal uses of veterinary drug products. Farmers are already almost all complying with this order.

2. Rewrite the sentences you identified above, placing the modifiers appropriately.

_____

_____

_____

_____

_____

_____

_____

_____

_____

_____

_____

Additional Modifier Exercises

Identify each sentence below as having a misplaced or dangling modifier and rewrite it, correcting the problem

1. Using primitive tools, scientists have discovered Cro-Magnon man was human.

    _____

    _____

2. Bob stunned the pit bull with a large flashlight.

    _____

3. Walking into the house's entryway, the lamp glowed warmly.

    _____

4. Please choose a magazine on the enclosed card.

    _____

5. Sue found an emerald woman's bracelet.

    _____

6. Approaching the city from the west, the sports arena is quite a sight.

    _____

Chapter 14 Parallel Construction

1. In the following paragraph underline all parallel constructions and rewrite any nonparallel forms so that they are constructed in parallel form.

Recently, two pilots, one in a 175-seat commercial airliner and with the other one in a small, twin-engine corporate jet, were barreling toward each other. On the instrument panel of the commercial jet, a small air traffic screen flashed a yellow circle and a voice announced, "Traffic." As the yellow circle approached the center of the screen, it changed to a red square. The voice said loudly, "Climb, climb." Noticing the red square and as he pulled up, the pilot saw the other craft fly past several hundred feet below. The voice that called out the warning was not the copilot but the latest audiovisual aid to arrive in cockpits of planes, a traffic alert and collision avoidance system. The Federal Aviation Administration has issued an order that this system must be installed in 20 percent of all large commercial planes by next year and to install it in the rest of the large commercial planes using American airspace within the next three years. The system works by computing the distance between planes, warning planes when they get within six miles of each other, and then to decide which plane should climb and which should descend to avoid a collision.

2. Write a paragraph of at least five sentences in which there are parallel constructions in at least four of the sentences. You may want to write about air safety or airport safety.

_____

_____

_____

_____

_____

_____

_____

Chapter 15 Consistency (Avoiding Shifts)

1. The following paragraph has a number of inconsistent shifts in person and number, in verb tenses, in tone, in voice, and in discourse. Rewrite the paragraph on the lines below so that it avoids any inconsistent shifting.

High school proms used to be dances where students dressed up in suits and dresses and celebrated their coming graduation, but now you have to spend big bucks for a tuxedo or elegant formal dress. Proms have become big business as formalwear shops and limousine services offer their services in advertising campaigns. Tuxedo rental shops across the country report that proms, not weddings, account for the major proportion of its business. One local shop owner said that he used to look forward to summer as his busy season because of weddings, but now I make more money in the spring because of high school proms. The typical expenses now include the tuxedo rental, prom tickets, corsage, dinner, and limousine rental. You can easily spend $300 on the dance, and that was just for the basics. Promgoers can spend additional funds for the latest fashions in tuxes, and photos can be bought for $50 or more. Even when the prom is over, there were other expenses. Some kids go away for the whole weekend, often to a resort hotel. So you have to throw in the costs for a hotel, and if parents are along as chaperones, it is necessary to add in the cost of their rooms and meals too. High school graduates insist that this is all necessary as a rite of passage, but the expense is not appreciated by parents who often have to cough up at least part of the funds.

_____

_____

_____

_____

_____

_____

_____

_____

_____

_____

_____

_____

_____

_____

2. Write a paragraph of at least five sentences in which you pay special attention to consistency in pronoun person and number, verb tense, tone, and voice. You may want to write about high school proms.

_____

_____

_____

_____

_____

_____

_____

_____

_____

_____

_____

_____

_____

_____

_____

_____

Chapter 16 Faulty Predication

1. The following paragraph has some sentences with faulty predication. On the lines below, rewrite these sentences so that they are correct.

    With the present concern for the environment, some companies are trying to increase their sales by advertising their products as environmentally safe. The makers of some plastic trash bags, for example, are claiming that their plastic is degradable. The reason for the claim is because there are additives that cause the product to break down after prolonged exposure to sunlight. Biodegradability, they assert, is when there is photodegradability, a breakdown by sunlight. But since most trash bags are buried in landfills, the benefits of photodegradability are questionable. Thus, the government has stated that one way to improve deceptive advertising claims is when they eliminate false or misleading information.

    _____

    _____

    _____

    _____

    _____

    _____

2. Finish the sentences for each of the subjects listed here. Pay special attention to avoiding faulty predication.

    a   The reason is _____

        _____

    b   Horror is _____

        _____

    c   His excuse was _____

        _____

    d   Her proposal was _____

        _____

Chapter 17 Coordination and Subordination

The sentences in the following paragraph can be improved by adding more coordination and subordination. Rewrite the paragraph so that there is more coordination and subordination, but avoid excessive or inappropriate forms of adding clauses together.

Americans have become videotape addicts. Over 75 percent of all American households now have videocassette recorders, so hotels hope to make their guests feel at home by providing equipment for watching videotapes. Some of the largest hotel chains in the country have added videocassette recorders in the rooms which can be used by renting videocassettes from shops in the hotel where there is a good selection of recent movies for guests to view in their rooms. In these hotels guests can show their room key and can rent a movie at a reasonable rate. Other hotels don't want to bother with stores in the lobby, and they are exploring a different option, so they are adding automated video dispensing machines in their lobbies that hold hundreds of titles and have new releases as well as standard favorites. One hotel chain has a lot of large business conventions, and it has investigated another approach. It is offering to distribute to guests videotapes that the corporation holding the convention wants its participants to see since corporations like this because the videotapes can convey some of the key ideas being presented at the convention. Videotape players in hotel rooms may soon be standard equipment, just as television sets were added years ago when Americans became addicted to televisions so that they expected to watch televisions in their hotel rooms.

_____

_____

_____

_____

_____

_____

_____

_____

_____

Chapter 18 Sentence Clarity

1. The following paragraph has some sentences with clarity problems. Revise the paragraph to improve sentence clarity.

To jot handwritten notes onto an electronic pad may be a new approach to using computers. A special pen that projects a narrow light beam onto the pad is the way this is done. For computer users who have had to rely on entering data into a computer by means of a keyboard, it is a major step forward in using computers. Not having to type is less distracting to many people who are not skilled typists but whose computer usage is high. It has been the goal of computer developers to rid the computer of keyboards for the last twenty-five years. But there has been insufficient development in the field of character recognition as this is necessary for the elimination of keyboards. Teaching computers to read through optical character recognition is one way to eliminate the keyboard. Recognition of the human voice is another way for computers to cease to rely on keyboard inputting of data. Speech recognition is not advancing as rapidly as some computer developers would like, and it is not likely that the near future will see computers we can converse with. We hardly have not appropriate technology that is this advanced. More promising is the ability of the computer to scan images. Already character recognition machines are being used in offices where pages of printed material are scanned by machines. Also under consideration by computer developers are electronic gloves that could be used by people to point to areas of the screen. There is hardly no limit to what will be coming next in computer development. The doing away of the keyboard will result in saving time and in the elimination of all those typos.

_____

_____

_____

_____

_____

_____

_____

_____

_____

_____

_____

_____

_____

_____

_____

_____

2. Write a paragraph of at least five sentences in which you draw arrows from old information in sentences to new information. Use positive instead of negative, avoid double negatives, and pay special attention to using verbs instead of nouns. Underline any passive voice verbs and be sure that they are appropriate. You may want to write about your experience in using computers.

_____

_____

_____

_____

_____

_____

_____

_____

_____

_____

_____

_____

Chapter 19 Transitions

1. Rewrite the following paragraph by using transitions to build bridges between the sentences and parts of sentences. Use underlines to indicate the transitions added in your revised version.

My father really needs help. He is a workaholic. He works nearly twelve hours a day. Doctors have told him it is not only bad for his health, but it is affecting his family. He has worried my family to no end. My family has tried to help him. He has not acknowledged the problem. He has a tolerance that goes through the roof. He sneaks out of the house before anyone is awake. He gets home after most of us have finished dinner and are getting ready for bed. He works at home. His computer is connected to the one at his office. His work calls him at home. He has a pager and a cell phone. Things may be getting worse. Dad accepted a promotion to regional director.

_____

_____

_____

_____

_____

_____

_____

_____

_____

_____

_____

_____

_____

_____

_____

2. Write a paragraph of at least five sentences in which you use transitions in at least four of the sentences. Underline your transitions. You may want to write about your experience with delays in grocery store checkout lines.

_____

_____

_____

_____

_____

_____

_____

_____

_____

_____

_____

_____

_____

_____

_____

_____

_____

_____

_____

Chapter 20 Sentence Variety

1. The following paragraph has very little sentence variety. Revise the paragraph by using a combination of strategies to add variety.

      Animal rights activists are known primarily for their campaigns against fur coats and the use of animals in laboratories. They are also campaigning against rodeos. Protesters say that rodeo animals are being mistreated. They say the animals are starving and live a life filled with pain and suffering. Animal rights activists also say that rodeo horses buck because they are in pain. Rodeo and circus owners say that this is not so. These animals are well fed and comfortable. These animals would be going to slaughter if they were not used as show animals. Handlers explain that they have a healthy respect for the size and power of these animals. The animals are treated like star athletes. They enjoy performing. Animal rights activists point to the use of cattle prods and bucking straps to get the animals moving. Rodeo owners argue that even ranchers have to use electric prods to get herds moving. Ranchers used pitchforks before prods were used. Calf roping is also condemned by animal rights activists. Roping breaks calves' necks and can also snap vertebrae and legs. Calf roping has been banned in some states. Eliminating calf roping can result in the overall elimination of rodeo shows. Rodeo owners protest that breaking of calves' necks, bones, and vertebrae just doesn't happen. Rodeo owners invite activists to come to rodeos and see for themselves.

_____

_____

_____

_____

_____

_____

_____

_____

_____

_____

2. Find a paragraph you have written previously that you think needs more sentence variety. Rewrite the paragraph here so that you have combined sentences; added words, phrases, or clauses at the beginning of the sentence; or changed some sentences to dependent clauses within the sentence.

_____

_____

_____

_____

_____

_____

_____

_____

_____

_____

_____

_____

_____

3. The sentences in the following paragraph are all short, simple sentences, so the paragraph is choppy and unsophisticated. Improve the style and sense of the paragraph by adding sentence variety, combining the sentences with coordination and subordination, and adding transitions as needed.

Gardening can be a worthwhile activity. The gardener can produce food for her family. She can also help to save the environment and prevent the overuse of landfills. One way to do this is by mulching. Mulching is actually recycling. The gardener can recycle grass clippings and leaves. The clippings are from mowing the yard. The leaves have to be raked in the fall. The clippings and leaves are usually gathered in plastic bags. The bags are taken to the landfill by the waste collection companies. The gardener can use scraps from the kitchen. These scraps are usually discarded into plastic garbage bags also. The gardener can collect clippings and leaves in a corner of the garden. She can add scraps of food to the clippings and leaves. She can mix these all together to provide organic mulch. This mulch can be spread on the garden. The mulch will provide nutrients for the soil. The nutrients will cause the garden to produce bigger and better vegetables. The gardener reaps many rewards from her activities.

_____

_____

_____

_____

_____

_____

_____

_____

_____

_____

_____

_____

_____

_____

_____

_____

_____

_____

_____

_____

_____

_____

PART FIVE
PARTS OF SENTENCES

Chapter 21 Verbs

21a. Verb Phrases

1. Underline the verb phrases in the following paragraph.

        Some scientists are saying that a buildup of carbon dioxide and other greenhouse gases in the atmosphere will cause global warming. But another group of scientists argues that we should study the data more carefully before any firm conclusions are drawn. While scientists generally agree that an unchecked accumulation of greenhouse gases will cause changes, no one knows when it will start, how much will happen, or how rapidly it will occur. The most widely accepted estimate is that there will be a rise in the earth's average temperature as early as 2050. This could bring rising sea levels and severe droughts in some areas. But no one knows yet how clouds and the ocean's ability to absorb heat will affect this. When scientists understand this better, projections can be revised.

2. Write a paragraph of at least five sentences, and underline the verb phrases. You may want to write more about the greenhouse effect and global warming.

_____

_____

_____

_____

_____

_____

_____

21b. Verb Forms

1. In the following paragraph, underline verb forms that are part of a verb phrase with one line and verb forms that are used alone with two lines.

The evidence that global warming has started is not very strong. Some scientists believe that the concentration of carbon dioxide has increased over 25 percent since the early 1800s, but other scientists point to the fact that the average global temperature has risen by no more than a half degree Centigrade. Even that rise is questionable since there was a cooling period from 1940 to 1970 that caused forecasters to predict a return to the ice ages. Therefore, to act on predictions by passing laws that restrict or ban the use of fossil fuels may be hasty, but conserving energy, banning harmful chlorofluorocarbons, and planting more trees to absorb carbon dioxide from the air seems sensible. Many industries are also acting more responsibly and are reducing hazardous emissions from their factories.

2. Write a sentence using each of the following verb forms not as a part of the verb phrase but elsewhere in the sentence.

   a. -ing verb

   _____

   _____

   b. -ed verb

   _____

   _____

   c. to + verb

   _____

   _____

21c. Verb Tense

1. Underline the correct verb tenses from the choices given in the following paragraph.

In 1987, the FBI (opened, has opened, was opening) a $1.5 million mock-up of a small town in Virginia named Hogan's Alley. Presently, the town's population (has been, will be, is) about 200. Generally, Hogan's Alley (has looked, looks, is looking) like any peaceful little American town, but often the quiet (will be shattered, is shattered, had been shattered) by the sound of a shotgun or squealing tires. Then prospective G-men who (had been sitting, sat, will sit) outside the post office jump in their cars and race after the "criminals." None of this (will be, is, is being) real because Hogan's Alley (is, has been, had been) a training academy for those who (will want, want, will have wanted) to become FBI agents. Next year over 500 trainees (will have attended, attend, will attend) classes in frisking, lectures on handcuffing, and seminars on interrogating witnesses. The FBI (started, was starting, had started) Hogan's Alley because it wanted its agents to have more true-to-life experience before they go out and deal with dangerous criminals. So now every day there (will be, have been, are) mock bank robberies, kidnappings, and drug busts. The "criminals," however, are actors, part-time students, retirees, off-duty policemen and firemen, and anyone else who (has passed, will pass, had passed) the rigorous screening tests.

2. The following paragraph is written in present tense. At the beginning of the paragraph, add the words "Last year" and change the verbs in the rest of the paragraph so that it is in past tense. Be especially careful when changing irregular verbs.

In Hogan's Alley, the FBI's mock-up village for prospective FBI agents, the trainees take part in an intensive 14-week training course. About 46 agents move through the program which begins with lessons in surveillance. Trainees track a suspect from his home as he drives to a shopping mall and sells a small bag of phony cocaine. Next comes a class in simple arrests, when agents-in-training burst into a fleabag motel and take an unarmed burglar as he lies in bed. Agents learn how to frisk suspects, and then they read them their rights. Instructors, who bring their own experience as former FBI agents to the teaching, carefully give advice to each trainee and provide pointers on how to handle details such as slipping on handcuffs during a struggle. Nine weeks into the course, trainees get some practice in arresting an armed felon. Their final lessons take place in a courtroom, where they face a team of actors who pose as a tough team of defense lawyers. Those trainees who do not flunk out of the course become FBI agents, and the actors, who play drug peddlers, burglars, and other felons, say that seeing what it is like being on the wrong end of the law reminds them that they do not want to become criminals themselves.

21d. Verb Voice

1. The following paragraph contains both active and passive voice verb phrases. Indicate the voice by underlining "active" or "passive" in the parentheses.

Like many cities built on a river, Kansas City is divided (active, passive) between two states. The biggest single municipality is Kansas City, Missouri, but over one-half of the population of the metropolitan area lives (active, passive) in various suburban cities on the Kansas side. Problems are created (active, passive) when it comes time to finance projects that will benefit (active, passive) both sides of the state line. In the 1990s, cities on both sides of the state line agreed (active, passive) to a bi-state sales tax to be used to renovate Kansas City, Missouri's Union Station. Advocates said (active, passive) the new station would bring (active, passive) in tourism that would benefit both sides of the state line. Opponents claimed (active, passive) Kansas City, Missouri, was just trying to dip (active, passive) into the pockets of the more affluent suburbs on the Kansas side. In the end, a compromise was reached (active, passive). The bi-state sales tax was passed (active, passive), but all contributing cities had (active, passive) a say in its use and the tax had (active, passive) a 5-year duration. It was not renewed (active, passive).

2. Examine the sentences in the previous paragraph that you identified as having passive verbs. Rewrite them so that the verbs are in active voice or explain why the passive voice is more appropriate and less awkward.

_____

_____

_____

_____

_____

_____

_____

_____

3. Write a brief paragraph with at least five sentences in which you appropriately use three or more active verbs and appropriately use two or more passive verbs. Underline the active verbs once and the passive verbs twice. You may want to write about American inventions that interest you.

_____

_____

_____

_____

_____

_____

_____

_____

_____

21e. Verb Mood

1. Some of the verbs in the following paragraph are declarative (express a fact), some are subjunctive (express some doubt or something contrary to fact), and some are imperative (express a command). Underline the mood used for each.

Singles bars and dating services are thriving (declarative, subjunctive, imperative), but there are always new approaches. In commercial dating services, one new approach that may be cheaper (declarative, subjunctive, imperative) than the standard videotaped interviews is the lunch-date service. For less than $50 a month, the company promises (declarative, subjunctive, imperative) three lunch dates a month. People are paired on the basis of simple criteria gathered from brief interviews that might last (declarative, subjunctive, imperative) less than five minutes. The company sets up the lunch date, and the participants take it from there.

"Meet (declarative, subjunctive, imperative) new people," says the advertising brochure, "and enjoy (declarative, subjunctive, imperative) some interesting little restaurants." Since the Census Bureau puts (declarative, subjunctive, imperative) the number of single adults at 66 million and growing, these new twists on dating services may prosper (declarative, subjunctive, imperative).

2. Write sentences using each of the verb moods listed below.

a. declarative

_____

_____

b subjunctive

_____

_____

c. imperative

_____

_____

21f. Modal Verbs

1. The following paragraph includes modal verbs that express ability, a request, or an attitude (such as interest, expectation, possibility, or obligation). Underline the correct meaning from the choices given in parentheses after the modal verbs.

When American products began appearing in Moscow, city officials worried that the signs and advertising for these products might make (intend to make, could possibly make, need to make) Moscow look less Russian. A law recently passed in Moscow warns that all stores and businesses must display (are capable of displaying, expect to display, need to display) signs in Russian or at least change them into the Cyrillic alphabet. This has caused many businesses to contact the city inspector because of questions they have. For example, one businessman wondered whether he should change (has the ability to change, asks to change, is obliged to change) the letters in the label for the Puma running shoes that he sells. He was concerned that changing the letters from English to Russian might make (has the possibility of making, intends to make, requests to make) the shoes less well-known. The problem became confusing because the new law does not forbid foreign words but does require the Russian sign to be bigger than the one in English. Different stores found different solutions. An American cosmetics company, Estee Lauder, announced that they will put (are capable of putting, strongly intend to put, are asking permission to put) one sign with the Russian alphabet on their awning and another sign with the English alphabet in the windows. Despite all the questions and worries, the inspector in charge of enforcing this rule will be very strict about checking on foreign signs.

2. Write a brief paragraph with at least five sentences in which you use four or five modal verbs (shall, should, will, would, can, could, may, might, must, ought to). Underline each modal verb that you use. You may want to write about problems in translating words from one language to another or about the difficulties of having to use the English alphabet to write words from a language that uses a different alphabet.

_____

_____

_____

_____

_____

_____

_____

_____

_____

Chapter 22 Nouns and Pronouns

22a. Nouns

1. In the following paragraph, make the necessary corrections to the nouns that need the appropriate -s and -es plural noun endings and to the nouns that are missing possessive markers. Underline your corrections.

Sports fanatics are spending large sums of money these day to purchase sports memorabilia. In fact, says one of the industrys spokesperson, it is a $100 million-a-year obsession. Buyers look for scorecards, stadium seats, autographed baseball bats, and even children clothing that belonged to old-time greats such as Babe Ruth. Ruth personal letter to a fan recently sold for over $7000. Since Joe Lewis, the famous boxer, kept many of his old mouthpiece, collector are paying over $2000 for boxed sets of Lewis's mouthpieces. There is even a magazine entitled *Sports Collectors Digest* which keeps collector informed about many of the auction and the availability of various item of interest. A faculty member in the history department of a major American university has begun a study of this phenomenon and reports that yearly increases in prices are staggering. For example, he says, a nineteenth-century baseball card of an obscure Hall of Fame pitcher, Tim O'Keefe, which was worth about $750 two year ago, recently sold for over $30,000. O'Keefe's other memorabilia are expected to soar in value as well. Sports collectible are now big business.

2. Write a paragraph of at least five sentences and include nouns with -s and -es plural endings and nouns with correct possessive markers. Underline each such noun that you use. You may want to write about collecting sports memorabilia.

_____

_____

_____

_____

_____

_____

22b. Pronouns

In the following paragraph, underline all the pronouns, including the personal pronouns, demonstrative pronouns, relative pronouns, interrogative pronouns, indefinite pronouns, possessive pronouns, reflexive pronouns, and reciprocal pronouns.

The business of sports collectibles has become so profitable that it has attracted con artists who manage to forge and sell bogus items. The forgeries have become such big business, in fact, that many con artists help one another and have developed a large network of bogus items. These items include fake Joe DiMaggio signatures and imitation press box pins. Anyone who is in the memorabilia business can spot these forgeries and fakes, but sports fans are often too enthusiastic about a purchase to take the time to have their purchases checked by experts. As a result, they often allow themselves to be conned. A lot of junk from people's attics is also cluttering the market. When someone finds yellowed pages from 1929 sports sections in her scrapbook, she may think she has an expensive treasure. Flea markets overflow with these antiques which may or may not be worth anything. But if a buyer is willing to pay large sums of money, who can say whether that autographed photo or threadbare jersey is or is not a treasure worth collecting? With a market where buyers pay $20,000 for one of Lou Gehrig's old bats, it is worth cleaning out those old attics and scrapbooks.

Chapter 23 Pronoun Case and Reference

23a. Pronoun Case

1. In the following paragraph, underline the correct pronoun in the parentheses.

When historian Page Smith began to ask himself just what kind of education was being provided by American universities, he started with a list of questions. (His, His') answers can be found in (his, his') book entitled *Killing the Spirit.* (Them, Those) readers looking for encouraging conclusions will not find (they, them) in this report as Smith criticizes professors' lack of interest in teaching and (their, theirs, their') tendency to spend too much time writing books and articles that do not contribute anything useful to mankind's betterment. Smith finds (them, those) academics who look down on teaching as less important than research to be at fault. For (he, him), the student revolt of the 1960s and early 1970s was a time when students were looking for answers to important questions but got no help from their professors. There was no dialogue between their professors and (they, them) that addressed questions about meaning and values in life, says Smith. However, community colleges and small, independent colleges still concern (theirselves, themselves) with the needs of students. University administrators (who, whom) are more interested in budgets and specific agendas will not find answers in Smith's book, and readers will wonder (who, whom) his real audience is. To (who, whom) should (we, us) look for answers?

2. Write your own sentences below correctly using the pronouns listed.

   a. them

   _____

   _____

   b. whom

   _____

   _____

c. his

d. yours

e. theirs

f. ours

g. her

h. me

i. who

j. your

k. us

_____

_____

l. I

_____

_____

3. In the sentences below, underline the correct pronoun.

Fall break was over, and the research assignment was due the next day, so Ross asked Lucy if she wanted to go to the library with Amy and (he, him). The instructor had told the class that the students (who, whom) made high grades on the midterm exam would be those (who, whom) had read the assignments and completed all the homework. When the girls and (he, him) reached the reference room, they saw several classmates (who, whom) they could work with. They asked their friends, "(Who, Whom) has finished the assignment?" They were surprised that all the other students were finished and headed to Starbucks. It was clear that a long night lay ahead for the girls and (he, him). The next day, Ross asked the teacher, "Please give Lucy, Amy, and (I, me) one more day to finish the research assignment." But the teacher said it wouldn't be fair to the rest of the students (who, whom) had all worked hard, so Ross and (they, them) learned, yet again, not to procrastinate.

23b. Pronoun Reference

1. In the following paragraph there are some pronoun reference problems. Underline all the pronouns that do not clearly or correctly refer back to specific nouns.

When Benjamin Franklin discovered electricity in thunderclouds, he sparked a controversy that still has no clear answer. How do clouds become electrified in the first place? To this day they haven't been able to adequately explain how it contains such incredible amounts of electricity that a stroke of lightning can contain about 100 million volts. One researcher who wants to find some answers flies his plane into storms to measure electric fields and ice particle changes. It's bumpy work, he says, especially if there are large hailstones because it can damage the plane and the measuring equipment. On one trip they noticed that in sections of clouds where water and ice mix, the measuring devices picked up indications of strong charge separation. The answer may be that in a certain temperature range, the temperature can cause the charge separation. Another factor may be a kind of soft hail called "graupel," pea-sized particles that can look like miniature raspberries. They form when droplets of supercooled water collide, freezing together instantly. Ice crystals then bounce off the growing graupel, building up a charge from the friction just as you build up a static electricity charge when you scuff your feet across the carpet. When they are carried to different parts of the cloud, the result is a separation of the positively and negatively charged particles. Then, when the electrical difference between the ground and the sky becomes great enough, everyone should haul his or her kite in.

2. On the spaces below, rewrite the sentences from the paragraph above that have pronoun reference problems so that all the pronoun problems are eliminated.

_____

_____

_____

_____

_____

_____

_____

_____

_____

_____

_____

_____

_____

_____

3. Write a paragraph of at least five sentences with correctly used pronouns in every sentence. Underline each pronoun and draw an arrow back to the noun to which it refers. You may want to write about electricity or thunderstorms.

_____

_____

_____

_____

_____

_____

_____

_____

_____

Chapter 24 Adjectives and Adverbs

24a. Adjectives and Adverbs

1. In the following paragraph, underline all the adjectives and adverbs and correct the errors in adverb and adjective forms by writing the correct form above the line.

    For many people, the crossword puzzle in the daily paper is one of life's little pleasures. Some say it is also sureone of life's frustrations. While puzzle books conveniently include the answers in the back, most newspapers print the answers the next day. Now there is a more quicker answer. Some companies have an automated solution. Readers can dial an 800 service for instant answers. This service is free to callers but is paid for by advertisers who sponsor each day's puzzle. An advertiser can run a small advertisement by the puzzle and can include a ten-second message that callers will hear before the answers are given. *The New York Times* handles this more differently. For their puzzles, callers pay for all requests for clues. These services are a major breakthrough for frustrated puzzle-doers who are used to waiting until the next day.

2. Write sentences correctly using each of the adjectives or adverbs below.

    a. nice

    _____

    _____

    b. nicely

    _____

    _____

    c. sure

    _____

    _____

    d. surely

    _____

    _____

e. used

_____

_____

f. good

_____

_____

g. well

_____

_____

h. rapid

_____

_____

i. rapidly

_____

_____

j. real

_____

_____

k. really

_____

_____

l. so

_____

_____

24b. A/An/The

In the following paragraph, articles (a, an, the) may or may not be needed before certain nouns. Underline the correct answer in parentheses. Notice that one possibility is that no article is needed; if that is the case, underline that option.

After winding down twenty miles of dirt road in Mtunthama, Malawi, (a, an, the, no article) visitors will come upon the well-kept lawns and gardens of (a, an, the, no article) Kamuzu Academy, one of (a, an, the, no article) Africa's most unusual schools. Here, on four hundred acres of well-trimmed lands is (a, an, the, no article) school dedicated to classical scholarship. (A, An, The, no article) school was founded by President Hastings Kamuzu Banda, the ruler of Malawi since it won its independence from (a, an, the, no article) British in 1964. Originally, Dr. Banda studied in (a, an, the, no article) South Africa, (a, an, the, no article) United States of America, and (a, an, the, no article) Britain, where he acquired (a, an, the, no article) medical degree and (a, an, the, no article) love of Latin and Greek, as well as a strong attraction to the classical emphasis of the elite British schools. When Dr. Banda returned to Malawi, he wanted to copy (a, an, the, no article) architecture and curriculum of Eton and other British boarding schools. Some critics in opposition to Dr. Banda say that (a, an, the, no article) academy is not appropriate in their country where ordinary schools often do not have (a, an, the, no article) textbooks and where more than two-thirds of (a, an, the, no article) population are illiterate. However, defenders of the school point out that the school is not elite in choosing its students. Children are accepted without regard to their family's wealth or position. Each year 35,000 students take (a, an, the, no article) exam to try to gain entrance to the school which accepts about eighty new students (a, an, the, no article) year. Once accepted, all students are required to take four years of (a, an, the, no article) Latin and four years of (a, an, the, no article) ancient Greek, along with (a, an, the, no article) English, (a, an, the, no article) mathematics, and (a, an, the, no article) history course about Africa. Most graduates go on to university and then take jobs in (a, an, the, no article) Malawi civil service.

24c. Comparisons

Write sentences in which you use the correct comparative form of the word listed for the items given.

1. comparative form: large

    items compared: two colleges

    _____

    _____

2. comparative form: large

    items compared: eight colleges

    _____

    _____

3. comparative form: exciting

    items compared: two movies

    _____

    _____

4. comparative form: enjoyable

    items compared: three books

    _____

    _____

5. comparative form: user-friendly

    items compared: all computer software programs tested

    _____

    _____

6. comparative form: good

    items compared: two music CDs

    _____

    _____

7. comparative form: good

    items compared: three music CDs

    _____

    _____

8. comparative form: bad

    items compared: all meals you have ever eaten

    _____

    _____

Chapter 25 Prepositions

1. In the following paragraph, underline the correct choice for the preposition that should be used.

Americans used to pour ketchup over so many foods that it was America's favorite condiment. Now salsa has replaced ketchup as the favorite (among, between) the two (at, in, on) American food markets. Salsa, which means "sauce" (at, in, on) Spanish, is defined as any fresh-tasting, chunky mixture, usually made with tomatoes, chilies, onions, and other seasonings. Although salsa used to be associated (to, with, for) Mexican and southwestern cooking, it is being used for a variety of foods not particularly Mexican. The popularity (of, about, to) salsa is apparently part of the current food trend as Americans become more interested (about, on, in) spicier foods. In 1988, only 16 percent of households (at, among, in) America bought salsa. (In, At, For) two years, that figure was up to 36 percent, and the market continues to grow (in, at, by) a very fast rate. A marketing information company notes that salsas and picantes—which are different (from, than) salsas because they are thinner—account (on, to, for) about two-thirds of this market, a category that also includes taco and enchilada sauces. As the market expands, so do the choices. The simplest salsas are based (about, around, on) chopped tomatoes and chilies, and the types of chilies determine how hot the particular type of salsa is. Cookbooks with a variety of recipes indicate the preference of some people to make their salsas (in, at, to) home. Salsas are one of the few popular snack foods that are fat-free or nearly so, and many are made without preservatives, two characteristics that may contribute (on, to, around) their popularity now that people are interested (about, in) eating healthier. Riding on this wave of popularity are the new fruit salsas, made with peaches, pineapples, and so on, and vegetable salsas, made with pinto beans, corn, and black-eyed peas. Other varieties will surely appear as the market expands (in, on, at) the future.

2. Write sentences in which you correctly use the prepositions listed.

    a. compared to

    _____

    _____

b. compared with

_____

_____

c. independent of

_____

_____

d. similar to

_____

_____

e. different from

_____

_____

Chapter 26 Subjects

1. In the following paragraph, underline the subjects of all the verbs.

   Because television viewers of sporting events like to follow the actions of specific players, a cable company in New York is trying out a new subscription service. If it is successful, it is likely to become available to everyone: Cable subscribers will be able to tune into a tournament and pick the player they want to follow. Using a wand similar to a TV remote control, viewers sitting at home will be able to switch from conventional network coverage to a camera that focuses solely on the preferred player. Instant replays and a list of statistics on selected pros will be other selections that the service will provide. This interactive technology will allow viewers to customize programming. While the present programming is only a test of the technology, some cable companies foresee customers being able to sign up for interactive television just like other cable services. When will this service be available for everyone? It is too soon to know for sure, but there is certainly a large demand for such services.

2. Write a paragraph of five or more sentences and underline the word or words that are the subjects of all the clauses in your sentences. You may want to write about television viewing, cable services, or active vs. passive television viewing.

   _____

   _____

   _____

   _____

   _____

   _____

   _____

   _____

Chapter 27 Phrases

1. For each of the following sentences, choose the letter which best indicates the function of the underlined phrase. Write the letter in above the phrase.

   a. subject of the sentence

   b. tells more about the subject

   c. is the verb phrase

   d. gives added information about the verb

   e. completes the subject

   f. gives added information about another element in the sentence

   1. Marketers <u>have been working on</u> ways to improve aerosol dispensers so that they do not spray the harmful propellant into the atmosphere.

   2. One new product, <u>an alcohol-free hair spray</u>, cuts emissions of chemical pollutants by roughly 60 percent.

   3. For its propellant, this new hair spray uses dimethyloxide, a <u>nondamaging chemical</u>.

   4. Reformulating a proven compound <u>can be expensive</u> for manufacturers.

   5. Another solution to the problem is <u>a propellant-free container</u> with a rubber expanding sleeve.

   6. <u>The rubber's propensity to contract</u> provides the pressure to produce a spray when the nozzle is pressed.

   7. This new spray dispenser is already being widely used <u>with great success</u>.

2. Write your own sentences with phrases that serve the functions listed here, and underline the phrases you have used fulfilling those functions.

   a. phrase that is the subject of the sentence

   _____

   _____

   b. phrase that tells more about the subject

   _____

   _____

c. phrase that is the verb phrase

_____

_____

d. phrase that gives added information about the verb

_____

_____

e. phrase that completes the subject

_____

_____

f. phrase that gives added information about another element in the sentence

_____

_____

Chapter 28 Clauses

28a. Independent Clauses

1. In the following paragraph, underline the independent clauses.

     If you are a magician and like highly structured organizations, you may want to join either the International Brotherhood of Magicians or the Society of American Magicians. If, however, you are a magician who lives in New York City and likes to gather informally with other magicians, you should visit Reuben's Restaurant on 38th Street and Madison Avenue any Saturday afternoon. There will be professional and amateur magicians sitting in the back room, and they will be swapping tricks or polishing their routines on each other. People come in with jumbo interlocking rings, decks of cards, and brightly colored scarves in their pockets. Some are doctors, professors, salespersons in shoe stores, tax attorneys, shipping clerks, or teenagers who are just learning the basics. Others are professionals who have appeared on *The Tonight Show* or in traveling circuses. They all share a love of magic, and they willingly sit and watch each other's routines because they know how valuable it is to keep practicing.

2. Write a paragraph of at least five sentences in which at least four sentences have more than one independent clause. Underline the independent clauses you use. You may want to write about magicians or magic.

_____

_____

_____

_____

_____

_____

_____

_____

_____

_____

_____

_____

28b. Dependent Clauses

1. In the following paragraph, underline the dependent clauses and identify them as adjective or adverb clauses.

There are an estimated 50,000 magicians in America. Most are amateurs who enjoy magic as a hobby. These amateurs often have elaborate equipment although their only audience is usually their friends and relatives. Some, however, specialize in the small card, coin, and rope tricks that are always popular. Purists call this intimate "close-up" magic the only real magic because it relies so heavily on a person's manual dexterity. Because people seem to prefer to be fooled face-to-face, this close-up magic is also offered by professional magicians who perform at birthday parties and trade shows. A psychologist who is also a magician says that when something is done under people's noses, it's more magical. It's much more elusive. The spectacular effects of magic done on television don't seem to impress people quite so much. Whatever the cause may be, amateur magicians will keep buying those sponge balls, decks of cards, special coins, and paper flowers.

2. Write a paragraph of at least five sentences in which three or more sentences have dependent clauses. Underline the dependent clauses. You may want to write about magic or magicians.

_____

_____

_____

_____

_____

_____

Chapter 29
Essential and Nonessential Clauses and Phrases

1. On the lines below, rewrite the following paragraph so that all the nonessential clauses and phrases are taken out of the sentence and put in a new sentence following the one they are in now. Identify the essential clauses by underlining them.

Music teachers in the elementary schools who want to teach classical music to their students now have a lot of materials to help them. The materials, which many students say are excellent, have been developed by a group of educators who want to introduce classical music appreciation programs in elementary schools. These programs, incorporating listening skills and information about themes, styles, and forms of music, are also being used to coach students for contests. Students seem to enjoy these contests, a new form of competition in many schools. Contestants are often asked to identify the main themes of familiar works such as *Nutcracker Suite,* the specific instruments being played, and the composers. Harder questions, ones that stump even the more experienced teams, are those that are asked about music the students have not studied in school. Not all the music that is studied in the music appreciation classes is classical. Sometimes jazz and non-Western music is added, though students also seem to enjoy studying classical music that they have heard on television commercials. Music teachers who have tried these programs are pleased with the variety of types of music students come to like and the quantity of music they come to know. These music appreciation programs, begun on a small scale in a few states, are expanding rapidly across the nation.

_____

_____

_____

_____

_____

_____

_____

_____

_____

_____

_____

_____

_____

_____

_____

2. Write a paragraph of at least five sentences in which at least three sentences have an essential clause and at least two sentences have nonessential clauses. Underline the nonessential clauses. You may want to write about studying music in school.

_____

_____

_____

_____

_____

_____

_____

_____

_____

_____

_____

Chapter 30 Sentences

1.   Identify each of the following sentences according to the letter which describes it.

   a. simple sentence (one independent clause)

   b. compound sentence (two or more independent clauses)

   c. complex sentence (at least one independent clause and at least one dependent clause)

   d. compound-complex sentence (at least two independent clauses and at least one dependent clause)

   e. incomplete sentence (does not have at least one independent clause)

____ 1.   In today's society many working people who are in their thirties or forties face the problem of providing

   care for both their children and elderly parents while they are at work.

____ 2.   Since children have less contact with older people than in previous generations, a growing number of

   programs are being designed to bring children and older people together.

____ 3.   Which will benefit both groups.

____ 4.   In some programs there are centers for child care next to centers for the elderly, and there are plenty of

   opportunities for visiting between the centers.

____ 5.   Including shared activities such as cooking and birthday parties and informal get-togethers for storytelling

   hours.

____ 6.   Psychologists point out that this kind of contact, even between old people and youngsters who are not

   related, can fill a void in young children's lives when they do not have a grandparent living near by.

____ 7.   In addition, companionship with children keeps older people from feeling isolated and lonely.

____ 8.   There is also a societal need for older people to transmit life experiences to younger generations.

____ 9.   Something that is becoming increasingly less frequent in our mobile society where children move away

   from their parents and raise families on their own.

____10.   Programs to link children and the elderly have been so successful that similar programs have also sprung up

   that link retirees with at-risk teenagers, and these programs are providing great benefits to the teenagers.

____ 11.   A group based in Washington, D.C., which is a coalition of national organizations representing old and

   young constituents, works to push goals of mutual interest to the two age groups.

2. Write sentences illustrating each of the following types of sentences.

   a. compound sentence

     _____

     _____

   b. simple sentence

     _____

     _____

   c. incomplete sentence

     _____

     _____

   d. complex sentence

     _____

     _____

   e. compound-complex sentence

     _____

     _____

PART SIX
STYLE AND WORD CHOICE

Chapter 32 General and Specific Language

32a. General Versus Specific Statements

For each of the following, expand upon your original sentence by answering the questions below it. Then, rewrite the sentence so that it includes some or all of the specific information you generated.

1. Favorite Food: What is your favorite food? Be as specific as you can; for example, instead of saying "ice cream," write down which flavor (e.g. "chocolate-chip cookie dough").

_____

How would you describe the taste?

_____

What memories come to mind when you eat this food?

_____

Why is this food better than other foods?

_____

Now write a single, grammatically correct sentence that tells what your favorite food is and why.

_____

_____

_____

2. Career Choice: Once you complete your education, what career do you wish to pursue? Again, be as specific as possible.

_____

What initially drew you to this career choice?

_____

_____

_____

_____

What goals in life do you hope to achieve through your career?

_____

_____

_____

_____

What other careers have you considered, and what factors have led you to settle on your current choice?

_____

_____

_____

_____

Now write a single, grammatically correct sentence that tells what career you intend to pursue and why.

_____

_____

_____

_____

3. Most Important Person: Who was or is the most important person in your life? Write the person's name and his or her relationship to you (e.g. grandfather, friend, etc.).

_____

How would you describe your relationship to this person?

_____

_____

_____

How has this person helped you?

_____

_____

_____

_____

What have you learned from this person?

_____

_____

_____

_____

Now write a single, grammatically correct sentence that tells who the most important person in your life is and why.

_____

_____

_____

_____

32b. General Versus Specific Words

The following paragraph contains some underlined general terms which need to be replaced by more specific terms. The paragraph also contains some underlined specific terms which need to be replaced by more general terms. Revise the paragraph by replacing these terms with more appropriate ones. Write your revisions in above the lines.

    People like driving up for fast food, and now so do their <u>animals</u>. A new fast-food industry has begun for drive-in dog food, and the menu is entirely for <u>spaniels and collies</u>. These new <u>things</u> offer treats to dogs with dog biscuits shaped to resemble food. The dog biscuits are made from foods that help keep dogs healthy. The biscuits are <u>flavored</u> so that dogs don't get tired of the same thing. Customers love the idea of <u>driving their</u> <u>trucks to</u> a doggy drive-in after picking up their own stuff. So far the menu has been limited to dog biscuits, but <u>some men</u> will come up with new ideas for better <u>bone-shaped biscuits</u> for dogs

32c. Concrete Versus Abstract Words

The following paragraph contains some abstract words that are underlined. Change those abstract terms to more concrete ones.

When hikers reach a stream, they often decide to cross where the <u>route approaches</u> the water. But this may not be the best place at which to cross. Water usually moves most swiftly at the narrowest part of the stream. So, hikers should instead look for another spot where the stream widens. Here the current often <u>has less velocity</u> and may be easier to walk through. When hikers are carrying a backpack, they should loosen the shoulder straps and hip belt before <u>immersion</u> so that they can toss off the pack <u>if</u> <u>difficulties occur</u>. Some hikers find that if they suddenly hit a depression in the streambed, the weight of the backpack can toss them off balance. Another aid to crossing a stream is a good hiking stick. It can serve as another leg, offering better balance when there are <u>dangerous elements present</u>. It is helpful to remove unneeded <u>clothing</u> before crossing a stream with a swift current because the water can drag against <u>wet outerwear</u>. The hiker should also take each step slowly and deliberately. The forward foot should be planted firmly before the rear foot is moved. Finally, the careful hiker never hurries across a stream.

Chapter 33 Conciseness and Wordiness

The following paragraph contains many words and phrases that are unnecessary. Rewrite the paragraph on the lines below so that it is more concise.

It is definitely true that, as we all know, the topic of telling time is one that is of great importance to us all. This paragraph will discuss here the topic of time in our daily lives and how the concept of time has changed over time through the ages. Time plays an important role in people's lives because it is the essential measure against which other measurements of great and necessary importance were made. For example, we know that we can see that we measure the heart rates of our bodies in terms of time, and we know that we measure how fast our cars travel in terms of time. We organize our days and nights into whole segments of time, such as days, hours, minutes, and seconds, and from the very earliest beginnings of civilization people have counted the passage of time in terms of counting sunrises and sunsets or the movements of the moon as well as the movements of the sun in the sky overhead. For many centuries there was speculation about the nature of time that was mostly a philosophical discussion of how people perceive time and experience the passage of time. But in the twenty-first century science of today, since the work done by Albert Einstein, physicists have now come to realize that time is a definite dimension of the physical universe. Time is a measure of motion in space, not just some philosophical or theoretical thing that exists in people's minds as a concept they think about. The work of Albert Einstein, who was a physicist, also showed that time is not an absolute thing and that there is no such thing as a unique absolute time. It is known that people used to think that any event measured in time would be seen to take the same amount of time. To give an example of what this means, people used to think that two good clocks which are in good, accurate working order would agree on the time interval that it takes between two events. But history books tell us that the discovery that the speed of light appeared the same to every observer, no matter how he or she was moving, led to the theory of relativity. Now we know that time is seen by everyone relative to the observer who measures it. Each observer who observes time can have his or her own measure of time as recorded by the clock that he or she carries. Clocks that are carried by different observers do not necessarily have to agree. This view that observers do not have to agree on the time interval is a very different view of time from the older view of time that it is an absolute thing. However, as shown here, even with this notion that time is not an absolute thing, we still in our lives today use time as a means of measurement.

Chapter 34 Passive Voice Versus Active Voice

Rewrite the following paragraph, changing the passive voice to active as often as necessary.

It was recently announced by a team of European astronomers that a new planet was discovered in our galaxy. The planet -- technically known as an "exoplanet" because it exists outside of our solar system -- has been given the rather dull name of "Gliese 581c," since it orbits the star Gliese 581. It has been observed that Gliese 581c has some unique characteristics that separate it from the other 220 exoplanets that have been discovered so far. For instance, it has been noted that Gliese 581c has a substantial atmosphere and is likely to have oceans: two things that are deemed essential by astrobiologists for life to evolve. Furthermore, it is thought to exist in the so-called "Goldilocks Zone," which means its orbit relative to its sun is ideal for supporting life. Best of all, it is not so far away that it would be assumed to be impossible for us to travel there someday: it is only 20.5 light years away, which, in astronomical terms, is not considered to be very far at all.

_____

_____

_____

_____

_____

_____

_____

_____

_____

_____

_____

_____

_____

_____

Chapter 35 Unnecessary and Inappropriate Language

35a. Clichés

Listed here are some word groups that many people regard as clichés. Try to think of a different way to express the same idea by writing a sentence using fresher language instead of the cliché.

1. white as snow

   _____

   _____

2. rain or shine

   _____

   _____

3. beat around the bush

   _____

   _____

4. easier said than done

   _____

   _____

5. big as a house

   _____

   _____

6. work your fingers to the bone

   _____

   _____

7. live happily ever after

_____

_____

8. first and foremost

_____

_____

9. to be turned on by

_____

_____

10. climb the ladder of success

_____

_____

35b. Pretentious Language

1. Listed here are some sentences that use what many people regard as pretentious language. Try to think of a different way to express the same idea by writing a sentence using plain English instead of the pretentious language. You may want to use a dictionary to determine the meaning of some words.

    a. I unquestionably ascertained that the oration I planned to deliver to the assemblage of students required considerable revision.

    _____

    _____

    b. I was rendered mute by the import of the situation.

    _____

    _____

c. Nathan is someone who is noted for his singularity.

_____

_____

d. I shall slumber anon and awaken refreshed to meet the challenges of the pristine day.

_____

_____

e. The lucidity of the discourse was the source of significant veneration.

_____

_____

2. The language in the following paragraph is pretentious and wordy and thus inappropriate for most audiences. Rewrite the paragraph so that the language is appropriate for the target audience of college students.

As the twenty-first century moves inexorably forward in America, institutions of higher learning are endeavoring to appeal to diverse student populations and provide unprecedented access to their resources by making education available in multitudinous formats. Scholars may pursue their studies in traditional classroom settings, or they may opt to complete an entire degree program without ever gracing a college campus with their presence by conducting all their coursework in the amorphous environment of the Internet. Courses that do not require the student's physical presence on campus are called online courses and are conducted in their entirety through institutional electronic facilities. The student who is contemplating attempting this medium of intellectual pursuit must carefully consider the personal requirements for success in the online environment. The prospective online scholar must be highly disciplined, with no propensity toward procrastination. He or she must possess an elevated sense of personal responsibility and an advanced reading level. The preponderance of evidence supports the contention that, contrary to the collective opinion of older adolescent computer literati, online pursuit of college credit is not facile and effortless. In point of fact, online classes will indubitably require a far greater investment of time and concentrated effort than traditional classes.

Nevertheless, earning college credit through an online course will culminate in augmented computer literacy as well as discipline-specific erudition.

_____

_____

_____

_____

_____

_____

_____

_____

_____

_____

_____

_____

_____

_____

_____

_____

_____

_____

_____

Chapter 36 Appropriate Language

36a., 36e. Standard English, and Colloquialisms, Slang Terms, and Regionalisms

Listed here are sentences that use some nonstandard words, colloquialisms, slang, and regionalisms. Try to find a different way to express the same idea by writing a sentence using standard words in place of the nonstandard and by using appropriate words in place of colloquialisms, slang, and regionalisms.

1. I ain't planning to take those kids to the circus.

   _____

   _____

2. Jason watched a sci-fi movie and then zonked out on the sofa.

   _____

   _____

3. Mark weren't planning to fight, but when Frank started to dis him, he decided he couldn't be a chicken.

   _____

   _____

4. I'm not uptight about the English exam, but I'm afraid I'm going to flunk the history exam.

   _____

   _____

5. Dad freaked out when he saw I had my tongue pierced.

   _____

   _____

36b. Levels of Formality

The following paragraph is written in a very informal tone. Revise it so that it is more formal and would be appropriate to print in a science news magazine intended for a general audience of reasonably well-educated readers.

Parents worried about their kids being grabbed by kidnappers have a new gimmick. Parents used to depend on taking photos with the old Polaroid or maybe getting a set of prints to stash in some computer file. But those methods aren't foolproof. Kids grow up and out of what they looked like in photos, and prints can be kind of hard to match. Now scientists bugged by not having a really foolproof way to nail a kid's identity have found a way that is looking good. Parents can get a sample of their baby's DNA material, which has great gobs of information about that particular kid. There's even a storage place set up for this in New Jersey. What's on file there, if someone wants it, is enough info to take a sample and match it against a hair, piece of skin, or even a couple of dots of blood. This is called DNA "fingerprinting," and it nails a kid's identity positively. What's really cool about this is that all the information from the genes stored at this place lasts as long as the person hangs around this planet—or longer. Grown-ups are pretty interested in getting themselves on file there too, especially those whose personal safety isn't high because of a dangerous job.

_____

_____

_____

_____

_____

_____

_____

_____

_____

_____

_____

_____

_____

36c. Emphasis

Parallelism: Using the chart below, brainstorm ideas about what does and does not constitute beauty. Then, write a single sentence where you state all the things beauty is and is not. Remember to use correct parallel structure and punctuation.

Beauty is ...   Beauty is not ...

Striking Language: Choose a word for Column A and Column B to fit into the following sentence:

_____ is like [a] _____:
(word for Column A)   (word from Column B)

_____.

Then, after the colon, provide an explanation of your own devising to show the relationship between the two words.

Example: Love is like homework: the harder you work at it, the more you get out of it.

Column A	Column B
Love	Candy
Truth	Bowling
Honesty	Hip Hop
Cheating	Shopping
Beauty	Television
Friendship	Homework
Anger	Flower[s]
Greed	Dog[s]
Wisdom	Driving
Courage	The Internet
Kindness	Baseball
Death	Coffee
Life	College

36d. Denotation and Connotation

1. Each of the following words has either a positive or negative connotation. Think of an alternative term that has the oppos
    connotation.

EXAMPLE

<u>devoted</u>   <u>obsessed</u>

a. notorious   _____

b. assertive   _____

c. right-wing   _____

d. orderly, well organized   _____

e. garbage collector   _____

f. pre-owned   _____

g. dirt   _____

h. fragrance   _____

i. economical   _____

j. big spender   _____

2. Some connotations are personal and not always shared by others. If you have personal connotations for any of the following terms, write them here.

a. lake _____

b. ice _____

c. summer _____

d. chemistry _____

e. automobile _____

36f. Jargon and Technical Terms

Listed here are some sentences that use jargon and technical terms. Try to find a different way to express the same idea by writing a sentence using easily understandable language for a general audience. You may want to use a dictionary to find the meaning of unfamiliar words and terms.

1. My doctor told me that the antibiotic he prescribed for the inflammation of my gastrointestinal tract is counteracted by over-the-counter cold medications.

   _____

   _____

2. The learning facilitator of our pottery-making class doesn't receive enough monetary remuneration.

   _____

   _____

3. Our supervisor has asked that we revisit the problematic situation and provide input to its resolution.

   _____

   _____

4. Each candidate promised to implement no new revenue enhancements.

   _____

   _____

5. The scientist was studying the ferromagnetic properties of various Paleolithic artifacts.

   _____

   _____

Chapter 37 Nonsexist Language

1. The following paragraph has some sexist language that can be revised. On the lines below, rewrite the paragraph so that sexist language has been eliminated, and underline all the changes that you make. You may need to make other changes in various sentences as well.

In many suburban housing developments built during recent decades there are homeowners associations that enforce housing codes on all the homeowners. The average owner in such a suburb may think that he is free to paint his house whatever color he likes or park any kind of car in his driveway, but that is not the case. Homeowners associations often have a lawyer who spends his days enforcing the laws enacted by these associations. The laws see to it that all the members abide by the group's standards of good taste. No plastic flamingos are allowed on the lawn, and every house painter who works in the suburb knows that he cannot use certain colors for house trim, such as bright pink or a gaudy yellow, because he has to follow community guidelines. When houses are built in new developments, there are usually restrictive covenants that force the buyer to join the association, whether he likes it or not. Even when someone challenges the laws, he usually loses as the covenants are legally binding. It all starts with the builder because when a builder builds, he wants to make certain that the land value for the community stays high so that he can continue to sell his houses at a good price. The builder often starts off as the chairman of the homeowners association so that he can guide the formation of the rules and regulations. In one wealthy Florida community there are even regulations for local government and civil servants, including dress codes for policemen, taxi drivers, and mailmen. The only challenges that have gotten through the courts are those that show some regulation discriminates on the basis of race, religion, sex, or other characteristics of the homeowner.

_____

_____

_____

_____

_____

_____

_____

_____

_____

_____

_____

_____

_____

_____

_____

2. Write a paragraph about a job you have had in college or in high school or about the career you hope to pursue when you have graduated from college. Write the paragraph in third person, not in first person, and include a description of the responsibilities and expectations of persons in that job. Avoid sexist language in your description.

_____

_____

_____

_____

_____

_____

_____

_____

_____

_____

_____

PART SEVEN
PUNCTUATION

Chapter 38 Commas

38a. Commas in Compound Sentences

1. The following paragraph contains some compound sentences that need commas. Add commas where they are needed, and underline each comma you have added.

    In 1977 the flight of the little airplane, the Gossamer Condor, did not look very impressive but it was indeed a historic flight. With wings of foam, balsa wood, and Mylar, the plane designed by Paul MacCready floated slowly and gracefully over the San Joaquin Valley and covered a mile or so in about eight minutes. What made it so historic was that the pilot was pedaling. The Gossamer Condor was only the first of MacCready's pedal-powered planes and two years later the plane's successor, the Gossamer Albatross, crossed the English Channel. Some people say that MacCready is really the brains behind these inventions but others feel that he receives undue credit for the work that others on the development teams do. However, MacCready was the first to use his observations of how birds fly so his supporters feel that he is the genius who made human-powered flight possible. Other inventors were taking the conventional approach of trying to reduce drag as much as possible because they thought this approach would be the answer. The approaches of other inventors were to streamline their aircraft or they tried to incorporate ways to increase the horsepower. Only MacCready applied the principle of vastly increasing the wing area and used materials to keep the overall weight down. The result was an aircraft that needed only the power output of a good bicyclist and the Gossamer Condor now has a place of honor next to the *Spirit of St. Louis* in the Smithsonian Institute's National Air and Space Museum.

2. Write a paragraph with at least five compound sentences that are punctuated correctly with commas. You may want to write about the development of the airplane.

_____

_____

_____

_____

_____

_____

_____

_____

_____

38b. Commas After Introductory Words, Phrases, and Clauses

1. The following paragraph contains some sentences with introductory words, phrases, and clauses that need commas. Add commas where they are needed, and underline each comma you have added.

Having won prizes with his first human-powered plane Paul MacCready went on to build a faster and more powerful pedal-powered plane, the Gossamer Albatross. In less than two years after his first success MacCready's second pedal-powered plane departed from Folkestone, England, in June, 1979, bound for France. Expecting the flight to take about two hours MacCready allotted just enough water for the pilot to drink. The flight team who prepared the plane and assisted the pilot on the ground waited several weeks for the kind of calm weather that was needed. Consequently the pilot took off, expecting to reach France before his endurance and the water gave out. But a head wind blew up soon after the pilot was aloft. An hour and a half later he was only two-thirds of the way to France, and his legs were cramping from all the pedaling. Because everyone was sure they had to give up the attempt the flight team was ready to hook a towline to the craft that would haul it ashore. Tired and about to give up the pilot knew he had to gain altitude to get hooked to the towline. As he climbed he found less wind and was able to press on. Almost three hours later the pilot touched down at Cape Gris-Nez, in France, a minute short of his theoretical exhaustion point. The Gossamer Albatross had crossed the English Channel, powered only by the pilot.

2. Write a paragraph with at least five sentences that have introductory words, phrases, and clauses correctly punctuated with commas. You may want to write about a strenuous sport or competiton you were in.

_____

_____

_____

_____

_____

_____

_____

_____

38c. Commas with Essential and Nonessential Words, Phrases, and Clauses

1. The following paragraph contains some sentences with nonessential words, phrases, and clauses that need commas. Add commas where they are needed, and underline the commas you have added.

After designing human-powered planes, Paul MacCready a prize-winning inventor went on to design a solar-powered plane. MacCready however realized that solar cells as an energy source for planes do not make any practical sense. But MacCready who had long sympathized with environmental concerns hoped to demonstrate that solar power has an important part in the world's energy future. Those who see solar energy as merely a minor source of energy for the future downplay the importance of such demonstrations. Others think solar power has simply not been adequately developed for practical use. The solar-powered plane that MacCready designed flew from Paris to the coast of England in 1981 cruising at 441 mph at an altitude of 11,000 feet. The plane called the Solar Challenger provided the stepping stone to MacCready's next flying machine the Sunraycer a solar-powered car.

2. Write a paragraph with at least five sentences that contain essential and nonessential words, phrases, and clauses correctly punctuated with commas. You may want to write about the future of solar energy.

_____

_____

_____

_____

_____

_____

_____

_____

38d-h. Commas in Series and Lists; Commas with Adjectives; Commas with Dates, Addresses, Geographical Names, and Numbers; Other Uses for Commas; and Unnecessary Commas

The following paragraph contains some sentences with correct comma usage and with some comma errors. Add commas where they are needed, omit unneeded or incorrect commas, and underline each change you make.

The Sunraycer which is a solar-powered lightweight car, was built to compete in the 1987 Race Across Australia. Designed by Paul MacCready the car won the race from Darwin to Adelaide, and is now in the Smithsonian Institute's National Museum of American History. With a total weight of 365 pounds the car has a power output of about 1.8 horsepower at noon on a bright day and it gets the electric power equivalent of 500 miles to the gallon. The Sunraycer which presently holds the solar-powered speed record of 48.7 mph averaged a little over 40 mph for much of the race. The car is so light, that when it made turns during testing it often seemed in danger of blowing over. The engineers who worked on the Sunraycer, ended up putting two little ears on the top. "We're not sure why they work" said one engineer "though they seem to help." In some ways the Sunraycer is not a prototype of electric cars for commercial use, because the Sunraycer has bicycle-thin wheels a driver's seat that requires the driver to lie flat, and very weak acceleration. However many of Sunraycer's features were carried over into the electric car developed by General Motors. Like the Sunraycer the GM car uses alternating current, and can therefore get better performance. If electricpowered cars become widely popular in the future Paul MacCready will feel that he had some small part in saving the environment.

38a-h Review of Comma Usage

Commas are used correctly throughout the following paragraph. On the lines below, explain why the commas in each sentence are necessary.

(1)At the turn of the century Howelton was a well-established community of family-operated small farms at the top of Little Sand Mountain in Etowah County, Alabama, between Attalla and Walnut Grove. (2)In this community Thomas Lee and Mollie Benson grew up. (3)He was born in 1888, the son of M.O. and Alice Lee, and Mollie was born to W.J. and Fanny Benson in 1891. (4)Both families were highly respected, hard-working members of the community. (5)Both Thomas and Mollie completed the seven grades available at the community school, which meant they were prepared to take their places in the community and to take on the responsibility of marriage and family. (6)Though a few would move to one of the nearby towns to get a job in public works, most young people would at that point become farmers. (7)Having been sweethearts for years, Mollie and Thomas were married on Sunday, January 31, 1909, when he was 21 and she was 18. (8)In that community at that time there were very few big weddings. (9)Usually the couple informed the minister that they wished to be married at the end of the morning service, and they had a simple ceremony with friends and family in the congregation. (10)Thomas and Mollie's wedding, however, was more memorable than most, as the church burned to the ground that afternoon!

1. _____

_____

2. _____

_____

3. _____

_____

4. _____

_____

5. _____

_____

6. _____

_____

7. _____

_____

8. _____

_____

9. _____

_____

10. _____

_____

Chapter 39 Apostrophes

1. The following paragraph contains sentences with some apostrophes incorrectly used to show possession, mark contractions, and indicate plurals, as well as some missing apostrophes. Add apostrophes where they are needed (even if they are optional), omit those that are unneeded or incorrect, and underline each change you make.

> In the game of baseball, batting slump's are one of a players worst nightmares. When they are doing well, player's attribute their successes to mysterious minor occurrences around them that then become habits' the players keep up. After a game in which one baseball player who was wearing an old helmet with it's side dented hit two triple's, a home run, and a single, the player continued to wear that helmet for the rest of the season. Warding off evil spirits through superstitions is another thing baseball player's do. One player always wears the green T-shirt from his university under his teams jersey. Another wont wear a jersey with any 6s in his players number. Batting coaches spend hours watching videotapes with slumping players, trying to find whats causing the problem. They examine the players batting stance or swing, but this does'nt always provide useful clues. Some slumps happen when batters begin to worry too much about their misses and about everyone elses successes. But one coach thinks otherwise. He notes that some players' start making adjustments when theyve hit a double and want to hit farther or when a certain unusual pitch connected well with their bats. Players in their 30s' complain of a different kind of slump. One bad day, says one over-30 player, may mean he is losing it, that his age has begun to take it's toll. A hitter who is hot, on the other hand, tends to get possessive about a special bat and uses it until it breaks or its' cracks begin to show. When that bat goes, the player sometimes loses confidence until he connects with a new bat that brings him a few homerun's. A batters life is'nt as easy as some people think it is.

2. Write a paragraph with at least five sentences that use apostrophes correctly. You may want to write about the performance slumps of professional athletes or teams or about low periods or slumps in your life.

_____

_____

_____

_____

Chapter 40 Semicolons

1. The following paragraph contains some sentences that need semicolons and some sentences with incorrectly used semicolons. Add semicolons or change punctuation marks to semicolons where they are needed, delete those that are incorrect, and add correct punctuation, if needed. Underline each change you make.

       Junk mail used to be confined to print on paper, now it is appearing in people's mailboxes on videocassettes. Companies in the direct-mail business are now marketing inexpensive cardboard videocassettes that can carry a variety of messages; such as audiovisual advertisements, promotional premiums, and educational or training aids. Some companies are switching to this form of direct-mail advertising because it is relatively cheap, in addition, it presents messages more vividly on television screens than print advertising can on paper. Informational videos can be sent to prospective customers, and advertisers can use their product in the video. Says the spokesperson for one cereal company, "We are interested in promoting good nutritional habits;" as might be expected, the balanced diet they will be picturing in the video will include their cereal. Printed instructions on merchandise are often confusing, consequently, some manufacturers are also switching to these disposable videocassettes for the instructional packets they include with their merchandise. The cardboard videocassettes are relatively cheap to manufacture and cheap to mail. They are certainly more convenient than the promotional packets sent by companies that have relied on enclosing sample packets of toothpaste, aspirin, or cereal, mail advertisers who send bulky envelopes of coupons, and companies who want to entice customers with big brochures of vacation places, hotels, and tours. The disposable videocassette is certainly going to grow in popularity as an advertising medium.

2. Write a paragraph with at least five sentences using semicolons in compound sentences and lists. You may want to write about junk mail.

_____

_____

_____

_____

_____

_____

Chapter 41 Colons

1. The following paragraph contains some sentences that need colons and some sentences with incorrectly used colons. Add colons or change punctuation marks to colons where they are needed, delete those that are incorrect, and add correct punctuation, if needed. Underline each change you make.

Evaluating college teachers is a complex, often difficult task. Now a new method devised in the Midwest is being tried out across the nation the teaching portfolio. Administrators and faculty members see the portfolio, a collection of materials documenting classroom performance, as a way to emphasize teaching as a major priority. Too often, professors who are being evaluated document primarily their research and scholarly activities, such as: published books and article, lists of grants, and conference presentations. Says one faculty member at a large Eastern university, "When it comes to teaching, most teachers only have student evaluations and coffee-room conversations about what they do in class and how their students are learning": this kind of evidence is not very thorough or sufficient to determine pay raises, tenure, and promotion. As a result, many faculty members are judged and rewarded on the basis of their research and publications. Their teaching performance, whether outstanding or mediocre, is largely ignored. The portfolio can be a better measure of what faculty really do as teachers, for the portfolio can consist of the following items: a statement of the person's teaching philosophy, a list of the courses that person has taught, a representative syllabus, statements by fellow faculty members who have observed this person, and course materials that the person has prepared. At some schools where portfolios are already in use, the portfolios also include: unsolicited letters from former students, teaching awards, and even videotapes of the candidate teaching a class. Some faculty members who have prepared these portfolios say that there is an added advantage, the portfolio collection can lead to self-improvement. This can happen when the process of creating the collection causes the person to think seriously about teaching goals, strategies, and results.

2. Write sentences using colons in each of the patterns below.

    a. Colon to announce an element at the end of the sentence

    _____

    _____

b. Colon to separate independent clauses

_____

_____

c. Colon to announce a long quotation

_____

_____

d. Colon in a salutation

_____

_____

e. Colon between elements

_____

_____

f. Colon with quotation marks

_____

_____

Chapter 42 Quotation Marks

1. The following paragraph contains some sentences with correct and incorrect use of quotation marks. Revise and add quotation marks, if needed. Write your changes in above the lines.

"Why am I fatter than my sister-in-law? I eat less, complained a woman being studied by a team of researchers. She explained that she "repeatedly went on diets when her sister-in-law didn't." But the woman continues to weigh more. Researchers are finding out that heredity, in addition to "lifestyle,î"exerts a strong influence on people's weight. By studying identical and fraternal twins, research teams are finding that brothers and sisters end up with similar body weights whether or not they are raised in different families. In the "Journal of Genetics," Dr. Albert Skinnerd writes, "When the biological parents are fat, there is an 80 percent chance that their children will also be overweight". (234). "Does this mean that my brother and I are doomed to be fat," asked one overweight twin in the study? Since some sets of twins tend to transform extra calories into fat while other sets of twins tend to convert extra calories into muscle, one scientist concluded that "genes do seem to have something to do with the amount you gain when you overeat". Some unsuccessful dieters may be relieved to know that their failed diets aren't a matter of failed "willpower." It is really a matter of metabolism", reports another doctor doing research in this field. But that does not mean that low-fat diets and exercise should be given up. Quit is not a word in my vocabulary", says one constant dieter who manages to maintain a reasonable weight by means of careful eating and plenty of exercise, despite a tendency to be overweight.

2. Write a paragraph of at least five sentences using at least five sets of quotation marks for direct quotations, minor titles and parts of wholes, words used as words, and other uses of quotation marks. You may want to write about dieting.

_____

_____

_____

_____

_____

_____

_____

_____

_____

_____

_____

3. Write a dialogue based on this situation: You and two classmates are discussing an upcoming exam in your American literature class. Include at least six separate speeches (two by each speaker, for example) and include titles of a short story, an essay, or a sermon; a poem; and a novel that may be covered on the test.

_____

_____

_____

_____

_____

_____

_____

_____

_____

_____

_____

_____

_____

_____

_____

_____

_____

Chapter 43 Hyphens
Chapter 44 End Punctuation
Chapter 45 Other Punctuation

1. The following paragraph needs one or more hyphens, dashes, slashes, parentheses, and brackets. Add those that are needed, revise any that are not used correctly, and underline all changes that you make.

Which oils are good for us to eat? A study of thirty nine participants on a reduced fat diet looked at the benefits of consuming olive oil and [or] corn oil. Which is more beneficial in influencing high/density lipoprotein levels corn oil or olive oil? This is an important question because high-density lipoprotein [HDL] is considered a beneficial form of cholesterol that helps remove the more dangerous low-density lipoproteins from the body. In a study published in an article, "Two Healthy Oils for Human Consumption" [*Diet and Health News* 14 (1991): 22ó36], researchers report that the participants first spent twelve weeks on a diet that included olive-oil and then another twelve weeks on a corn oil diet. The results (which were also announced on television newscasts) indicated that neither diet resulted in lower-levels of HDL. This indicates that a diet of olive oil and (or) corn oil can accompany a reduced—fat diet. For those who self-select the oils they use in their diet, the choice is probably a matter of taste-or cost.

2. The following paragraph contains some sentences with incorrect use of periods, question marks, exclamation points, and ellipses. Add or change these punctuation marks where they are needed, delete those that are incorrect, and add correct punctuation, if needed. Underline each change you make.

"Do you see that green area to the left of the river we are flying over"? said the pilot to the passengers as the commercial 747 jet flew over southern Texas. Continued the pilot, "That's my grandfather's ranch! I often visited there as a kid!" Public address systems in commercial planes are now being used by pilots to enliven their passengers' flights. Some pilots are opposed to this practice because they see it as a distraction. Says one seasoned veteran, "Our task is to fly the plane, not amuse the passengers". But others disagree. Interesting, informative comments can put nervous passengers more at ease and can shorten a long flight. For those pilots interested in making such publicaddress announcements, there is now a book put together by an ex-pilot which pinpoints more than 1,200 historical and little-known places of interest on a collection of highway maps of the U.S. The maps are overlaid with the flight paths used by commercial pilots. Are you flying between

El Paso, Texas, and Las Vegas, New Mexico. If so, then look for the site of the Berringer Crater, where a meteor hit with such force 22,000 years ago that it killed all animal and plant life within 100 miles! Thousands of these maps have been sold, with more frequent fliers than pilots doing the buying! 'We are learning…an awful lot about territory we thought we knew"! says one frequent flier who takes her book with her on every flight. Another customer reports, "I bought one for my uncle who hates airplanes, and he now actually enjoys his flights". The book is obviously a success! Is the author correct when he says, "Soon, there will be such books in the pocket of every seat in every commercial flight?

3. Write a paragraph of at least five sentences correctly using one hyphen, one dash, one slash, one ellipsis, one set of parentheses, and one set of brackets. Also use three different kinds of end punctuation correctly. You may want to write about commercial flights.

_____

_____

_____

_____

_____

_____

_____

_____

_____

_____

_____

_____

Part Seven Review

Copy a paragraph of eight to twelve sentences from a paper you have recently written or are now working on. Number and correctly punctuate every sentence. On the lines below the paragraph, write the number and provide a brief explanation for each punctuation mark in every sentence.

_____

_____

_____

_____

_____

_____

_____

_____

_____

_____

Explanation:

_____

_____

_____

_____

_____

_____

_____

_____

_____

PART EIGHT
MECHANICS AND SPELLING

Chapter 46 Capitals
Chapter 47 Abbreviations
Chapter 48 Numbers

1. Revise the following paragraph for correct use of capitals and abbreviations, as well as the correct way to write numbers. Underline all changes that you make.

One of Boston's most popular folk heroes is Paul Revere, whose Midnight ride was made famous in Longfellow's poem, "Paul Revere's Ride," in *Tales Of A Wayside Inn.* Not many tourists realize that many of the places mentioned in that poem are still part of Boston's Twentieth-Century landscape, along what is commonly called the Freedom trail. This well-marked Trail is actually a 2-mile line in red paint, bricks, or steps with 21 historic buildings, sites, and monuments documenting Boston's contribution to American history. 2 miles isn't long, but it usually takes tourists who are thorough 2 or 3 days to see everything on the trail. Most begin at the Boston common, the oldest public park in the U.S. Here colonists used the public land for grazing animals, training the militia, and staging Public executions. Immediately next to the Common is America's first public botanical garden, the Boston Public garden, famous partly because it was the setting for the well-known children's book, *Make Way For Ducklings.* Just across the Street, on Beacon Street, is another of Boston's famous sites, the Old State House, completed in Seventeen Ninety-Eight. Its cornerstone was laid by Samuel Adams in 1793. 1 block East on Beacon street and then 1 block south on Park street is the historic Park street Church on the corner of Tremont. Here the song "America" was first sung on July 4, 1831. The next stop on the Freedom Trail is the Granary burying Ground, a Cemetery on Tremont Street. Some of the greatest U.S. patriots, including Paul Revere, Samuel Adams, John Hancock, James Otis, etc, are buried here. Also along Tremont street, at the corner of School street, is King's Chapel, the first anglican church in Boston. After the revolution, it became the first unitarian church in the country, and its cemetery contains the graves of many other early notables, including William Dawes, Jr. and Gov John Winthrop. (it was Gov. Winthrop who headed the group that founded the Boston colony.) Also on School Street is the first public school in america, which later became the Boston public latin School. Rev Cotton Mather, Ralph Waldo Emerson, John Hancock, Benjamin Franklin, et al, were alumni of this School. These are only a few of the many sights along the Freedom Trail. Longfellow's poem says, "hardly a man is now alive who remembers that famous night and ride...." True, but the Freedom Trail helps visitors realize many of the events that led to our Nation's independence.

2. Write a paragraph with at least five sentences correctly using capitals and numbers. Also include abbreviations of numbers, measurements, and dates. You may want to write about history.

_____

_____

_____

_____

_____

_____

_____

_____

_____

_____

Chapter 49 Underlining/Italics

1. Listed here are titles and words that either need underlines (or italics) or quotation marks. In the right-hand column, write a "U" if the titles or words need an underline (or italics) or "Q" if the titles or words need quotation marks.

   a.. Newsweek (magazine)   <u>U</u>

   b. Gone with the Wind (movie)   _____

   c. My Next Adventure (book chapter)   _____

   d. Buffy the Vampire Slayer (TV series)   _____

   e. Moby Dick (book)   _____

   f. To His Coy Mistress (short poem)   _____

   g. The Case of the Lost Diamond (TV episode)   _____

   h. The Barber of Seville (opera)   _____

   i. Paradise Lost (long poem)   _____

   j. Copenhagen's Museums (magazine article)   _____

   k. Time (news magazine)   _____

   l. Sweet Birdie (song)   _____

   m. Civil Rights Revisited (pamphlet)   _____

   n. The Economics of Solar Energy (magazine article)   _____

   o. C (letter of the alphabet)   _____

   p. Jurassic Park (book)   _____

   q. Exxon Valdez (ship)   _____

   r. dejure (Latin phrase)   _____

s. My Nervous Childhood (essay)   _____

t. Washington Post (newspaper)   _____

2. Write a paragraph of at least five sentences in which you correctly use underlining at least five times. You may want to write about books, magazines, articles, television programs, and movies that you enjoy.

_____

_____

_____

_____

_____

_____

_____

_____

_____

_____

_____

_____

_____

_____

_____

Chapter 50 Spelling

50a. Proofreading

Proofread the following paragraph for spelling errors, typos, and omitted words. Use the dictionary if needed, and underline all the revisions you make.

Inventors of gadgets for automobiles havn't always been successful with there inventions. But we can see from some these inventions that people have been looking for ways to make cars more functional, better looking, and more fun to drive, for example, we now have elegent and sophisticated ways tohere music in ou cars, but some of the earlier ways to add music to driving seem a bit odd now. In the 1920's, Daniel Young recieved a patent for an organ he invented for use in automobiles. He built organ keyboards that could be attached to back of the front seat so that people ridding in the back could play the organ to entertain themselfs. This may have been a good idea, exept for one thing. The roads of that time, unfortunatly, were so bumpy and uneven that the sounds produced by the organ when the car was moving where anythhing but beautiful. Another terriffic idea that didn't make it was Leander Pelton's patent for a car that could be parked by standing it on end. Instead of a back bumpper, he buildt a vertical platform with rolers attached. When parking the Vertical-Park Car, the driver needed to tip the car back onto platform. Than he could just shove the car into any approrpiately sized space. To preform this task, however, was a big dificult as Pelton never quite explained how the car was to be tiped from horzontal to vertical and back down again. A diffrent problem was that Pelton didn't porvide any way to keep gasoline, water, and oil from spilling once the car was up on its parkking rollers. But the government gave him a patent; he simply couldn't get anyone to manifacture his VerticalPark car. Another invention that never made it was designed by Joseph Grant in 1926—an autombile wash machine. The machin didn't wash cars, but it suppossedly washed clothes. Grant's invention consistted of a tub and paddles that bolted to the car's runing boards. when the tub was filled with water, soap, and drity clothes, the bouncing of the car over rought roads provided all the power and agitatition necessary to clean a load of dirty clothes. For realy dirty load, an extra twenty miles or so of driving was reccommended.

50c. Some Spelling Guidelines

1. **IE/EI:** Using the rules for IE/EI spellings (and the exceptions), underline the correctly spelled words in these sentences.

   a. Does he really (beleive, believe) he will win the lottery?

   b. The soybean (yeild, yield) this year will be high.

   c. She knows how to (seize, sieze) the day.

   d. The (height, hieght) of that tree is unusual.

   e. The company is working hard to establish more (foreign, foriegn) markets.

   f. My (weird, wierd) brother is always trying some crazy new herbal diet.

   g. What is your (field, feild) of study?

   h. No more than (eight, ieght) people can fit in that van.

   i. He tried to (deceive, decieve) himself into thinking he was able to do that.

   j. She approached a (financeir, financier) to help her start a new business.

   k. We called off the party when (neither, niether) of the guests of honor could come to it.

   l. During the rainstorm, the (ceiling, cieling) leaked badly.

   m. When is your (neice, niece) coming to visit?

   n. Our new (neighbor, nieghbor) seems like a pleasant person.

   o. The nurse tried to find a (vein, vien).

2. **Doubling Consonants:** Underline the correctly spelled word in these sentences.

   a. I have to be quiet when my sister is (naping, napping).

   b. It was hard to keep my (footing, footting) on that slippery slope.

   c. Was that the movie that Paul Newman (starred, stared) in?

   d. As she listened to the music, she kept (tapping, taping) her fingers on the desk.

   e. To whom were you (writting, writing) that long letter last night?

   f. I hope she (referred, refered) me to a good dentist

   g. When I stubbed my toe, I (hopped, hoped) around moaning and complaining.

   h. It was a strange (occurrence, occurence) to see the sky lit up like that.

i. I came in at the (begining, beginning) of the movie.

j. They really (benefited, benefitted) from that study session before the exam.

k. My father hates to go (shoping, shopping) when heís on vacation.

l. The advertisement (omitted, omited) any mention of the price.

3. **Doubling Consonants:** Write sentences using the -ed or -ing forms of the words listed here in sentences.

a. shop

_____

_____

b. hope

_____

_____

c. tape

_____

_____

d. star

_____

_____

e. write

_____

_____

f. top

_____

_____

g. slip

_____

_____

h. omit

_____

_____

i. prefer

_____

_____

j. refer

_____

_____

k. benefit

_____

_____

l. occur

_____

_____

4. **Prefixes and Suffixes:** Correctly add the prefixes or suffixes to the words listed here, and then write a sentence using the word and its prefix or suffix. Consult a dictionary if needed to check on the spelling or the meaning of the word that is formed by adding the prefix or suffix.

a. actual+ly

_____

_____

b. ante + cedent

_____

_____

c. anti + biotic

_____

_____

d.   auto + biography

_____

_____

e.   bene + diction

_____

_____

f.   bi+ partisan

_____

_____

g.   desire + able

_____

_____

h.   de + value

_____

_____

i.   dis + agree

_____

_____

j.   im+migrate

_____

_____

k.   inter+mission

_____

_____

l. mis+ inform

_____

_____

m. mis + spell

_____

_____

n. notice + able

_____

_____

o. pre+form

_____

_____

p. per+form

_____

_____

q. picnic + ing

_____

_____

r. pro+nounce

_____

_____

s. real+ly

_____

_____

t. true + ly

_____

_____

5. **Y to I:** Correctly add the suffixes given to the words listed here, and then write a sentence using the newly formed word.

a. ready + ed

_____

_____

b. lonely + ness

_____

_____

c. carry + ed

_____

_____

d. carry + ing

_____

_____

e. bounty + ful

_____

_____

f. greasy + ness

_____

_____

g. play + ed

_____

_____

h. employ + ed

_____

_____

i. petty + ness

_____

_____

j. forty + eth

_____

_____

50d. Plurals

For each of the following words write a sentence using the plural form of the word.

1. apology

_____

_____

2. ceremony

_____

_____

3. box

_____

_____

4. city

_____

_____

5. sister-in-law

_____

_____

6. church

_____

_____

7. videocassette recorder

_____

_____

8. radio

_____

_____

9. basis

_____

_____

10. attorney

_____

_____

50e. Sound-Alike Words (Homonyms)

1. Underline the correct word in these sentences.

   a. Everyone came to the concert (accept, except) Tiana.

   b. Does that store (accept, except) personal checks?

   c. I think the horror movie he saw (affected, effected) his sleep.

   d. The horror movie had no (affect, effect) on him whatsoever.

   e. When her friend is visiting (hear, here), she never gets any studying done.

   f. (It's, Its) a cool, rainy day today.

   g. I wonder when (it's, its) going to get better.

h.   What is (itís, its) temperature?

i.   Last week (passed, past) so quickly, it seems.

j.   She is no bigger (then, than) I am.

k.   Leah stayed until her friend joined her, but (then, than) she left the party.

l.   What did they do (than, then)?

m.   All the speakers (there, their) vowed (there, their) loyalty to the union.

n.   I gave my red sweater (to, too) my sister since I have (to, too) many.

o.   They (were, where) on the right road, but they took the wrong turn.

p.   I never know (whose, whoís) right in those arguments.

q.   Kristen knows (your, youíre) right, but she will never say it to (your, youíre) face.

r.   Could you give me some (advice, advise) about (buying, bying) a used car?

s.   That is going to be the (sight, site, cite) for the new shopping mall.

t.   She was (quite, quiet, quit) sure that she had taken her wallet out of her purse.

u.   You have to keep the camera (stationary, stationery) when you take the picture.

v.   Everyone had (all ready, already) left when the music finally began.

w.   I guess itís (alright, all right) to charge that sweater to my motherís account.

x.   Perhaps you can use (anyone, any one) of the golf balls lying there.

y.   The kit to build that model comes (altogether, all together) with the tools you will need.

2.   Use the following words in sentences. Be sure that they are spelled correctly

a.   accept

_____

_____

b.   except

_____

_____

c. affect

_____

_____

d. effect

_____

_____

e. here

_____

_____

f. hear

_____

_____

g. its

_____

_____

h. it's

_____

_____

i. passed

_____

_____

j. past

_____

_____

k. than

_____

_____

l. then

_____

_____

m. they're

_____

_____

n. their

_____

_____

o. there

_____

_____

p. too

_____

_____

q. to

_____

_____

r. were

_____

_____

s. we're

_____

_____

t. where

_____

_____

u. who's

_____

_____

v. whose

_____

_____

w. your

_____

_____

x. you're

_____

_____

y. advice

_____

_____

z. advise

_____

_____

aa. site

_____

_____

bb. cite

_____

_____

cc. sight

_____

_____

dd. dessert

_____

_____

ee. desert

_____

_____

PART NINE
ESL AND MULTILINGUAL WRITERS

Chapter 51 American Style in Writing

If your first language is not English, write a paragraph describing how the writing style in your native language differs from the American style in writing. Issues you might consider in your paragraph include conciseness, topic announcement, organization, and source citation. If your first language is English, interview someone whose native language is something other than English, and write a paragraph describing how that person's writing style differs from the American style.

_____

_____

_____

_____

_____

_____

_____

_____

_____

_____

_____

_____

_____

_____

_____

_____

_____

Chapter 52 Verbs

1. The following paragraph contains some errors in the verbs. Underline the errors and write your corrections above the words you underlined.

When people from other countries will shop in American supermarkets, they find an amazing supply of items other than grocery items. On one aisle, a shopper will discovered, for example, toiletry items such as toothbrushes, toothpaste, deodorant, and shampoo. On another aisle be paper towels, garbage bags, and cleaning supplies. Sometimes the choices would be confusing. But the choices do not ended with the shopping itself. Even when the shopping have conclude, the shopper may have decisions to make. For example, the person behind the checkout counter may asked if the customer would want the purchases in a plastic bag or a paper bag. Of course, if Americans was to shop in stores and bazaars in other countries, they can find the process just as confusing.

2. In the following paragraph underline the correct form of the verb that is needed.

In the United States, students hope (to learn, learning) more than just the subject matter they are studying. They believe that if they (study, will study) a subject thoroughly, ask questions, and even (disagree, will disagree) with certain opinions of writers and scholars, they (will become, become) better thinkers as well. Students from other countries may find it difficult at first to practice critical-thinking skills in American classrooms because (to question, questioning) an authority or the written word may be a sign of disrespect in their country. Another problem that students from other countries may encounter in American classrooms involves writing assignments. Whereas American students are comfortable with (choosing, to choose) topics for writing that argue accepted ideas, students from other countries may have difficulty (to express, expressing) their opinions without (apologizing, to apologize) for them because (discussing, to discuss) controversial topics may be considered rude in their country. Obviously, students' cultural backgrounds affect many aspects of college life, including how they approach the educational experience.

3. Use the following verb forms in sentences of your own. If the second word can be separated from the verb in your sentence, a pronoun is included in parentheses.

a. should + verb

_____

_____

b. will be + verb

_____

_____

c. may + verb

_____

_____

d. can + verb

_____

_____

e. do + verb

_____

_____

f. may have been + verb

_____

_____

g. fall behind

_____

_____

h. get out of

_____

_____

i. look like

_____

_____

j. run across

_____

_____

k. tear (it) down

_____

_____

l. call(it)off

_____

_____

m.call (her) up

_____

_____

n. try (it) out

_____

_____

Chapter 53 Omitted Words

1. In the following paragraph there are omitted verbs and subjects. Revise the paragraph to conform to standard English by inserting verbs and subjects where they are needed.

When importing ivory became illegal in the United States in 1989, engineers and material scientists searched for substitutes for natural ivory. For piano makers, the ban on ivory brought on the problem of how to make piano keys after the supply on hand used up. While conservationists and elephant lovers want people stop using ivory, many pianists who have tested plastic substitutes about to abandon hope of having new pianos with satisfactory substitutes. However, may be a solution. A team of experts has produced a substitute that may satisfy many piano builders and piano players. This new synthetic ivory both resembles natural ivory and has a similar microscopic structure. But even with a substitute for piano keys now available, the market for ivory not decrease as piano makers never been major consumers of ivory. The largest consumers of ivory in the world are Asian manufacturers of signature stamps, but even have given up their use of ivory and switching to substitutes.

2. Write sentences beginning with the subjects listed below. Be sure to include all verbs that are needed.

    a. My English instructor _____

    _____

    b. The other students in my class _____

    _____

    c. In my country, students _____

    _____

    d. In most schools there _____

    _____

    e. The parents of the students _____

    _____

Chapter 54 Repeated Words

In the following sentences, underline the unnecessary words that repeat the subject, pronoun, or adverb.

a. Students in my class they are looking forward to the upcoming vacation.

b. The book that I wanted to read it was not in the library.

c. My teacher found the book that I left it in the classroom.

d. The apartment building where I live there has two swimming pools.

e. The child returned the dog that I had lost it.

f. The pie in the refrigerator it is for tonight's party.

g. The book drop where library books are placed there is full.

h. My aunt called on the new cellular telephone that she had it installed in her car.

2. Complete the following sentences being careful not to repeat the subject as a pronoun before the verb and being careful not to add unnecessary words when relative pronouns and relative adverbs introduce clauses.

a. Children in my family _____

_____

b. The computer that I want to buy _____

_____

c. The cat sat on the blanket that I left _____

_____

d. The car that I drive _____

_____

e. The girl who wants to borrow my notes _____

_____

Chapter 55 Count and Noncount Nouns

1. The following paragraph has both count and noncount nouns. Choose the correct form in parentheses and underline it.

   In American supermarkets, new (products, product) and (produce, produces) are constantly being added to the shelves. Children are attracted to new snack foods, and adults are frequently tempted to buy items with (information, informations) about health benefits. To increase consumer (confidence, confidences) in package labeling, the Food and Drug Administration has announced new (guideline, guidelines) for various claims food manufacturers add to their labels. Products that are advertised as "low (fat, fats)" have to provide (evidence, evidences) on the label and meet new government (standard, standards). For items that appeal to children, the amount of (sugar, sugars) must be clearly indicated. Particularly helpful are the new regulations on serving size because consumers in America have become very conscious of the amount of (protein, proteins) and (fat, fats) that they eat as well as the number of (calorie, calories).

2. Write a sentence for each of the words listed below. Some are count nouns, some are noncount nouns, and some have both a count meaning and a noncount meaning.

   a. research

   _____

   _____

   b. difficulty (as a count noun) and difficulty (as a noncount noun)

   _____

   _____

   c. table

   _____

   _____

   d. computer

   _____

   _____

e.light (as a count noun) and light (as a noncount noun)

_____

_____

f. truth

_____

_____

Chapter 56 Adjectives and Adverbs

56a-b. Order of Adverbs, and Order of Adjectives

1. Reorder the following word clusters to create correct sentences, being careful about the placement of the adjectives, adverbs, and nouns. Don't add any words, and be sure to capitalize the first letter of the first word in your sentence.

    a. new   eager   three   students   entered   quickly   the   classroom

    _____

    _____

    b. Japanese   favorite   food   her   is   sushi

    _____

    _____

    c. girls   the   young   were   frightened   easily

    _____

    _____

    d. sometimes   experience   I   homesickness   intense

    _____

    _____

    e. almost   forget   never   I   anniversary   our

    _____

    _____

2. Write a paragraph of your own correctly using at least three adjectives and three adverbs. You may want to write about learning to speak a second language.

    _____

    _____

    _____

_____

_____

_____

_____

_____

_____

_____

_____

_____

_____

_____

56c.-d. A/An/The, and Some/Any, Much/Many, Little/Few, Less/Fewer, Enough, No

1. In the paragraph below, underline the correct word in parentheses.

In northern India there is (a, an) conflict between wildlife officials and Gujjar herders of water buffalo.

(A, An, The) Indian government wants to turn the area into a national park, to be called the Fajaji National Park,

but for the last ten years, local water buffalo herders refuse to move off the land. The Gujjars keep herding their

water buffalo, despite warnings that the animals are eating up too (much, many) of the vegetation and that soon

there will be (less, few) areas that have not been destroyed by the herding. Several decades ago, the Gujjars

agreed to migrate every summer to give the forests a chance to grow again, but communities in the areas they

migrated to refused to accept the Gujjars because they needed (a, an, the) land for their own grazing, and they

didn't have (fewer, enough, no) land to share. As a result, the Gujjars now stay in the forest throughout (a, an,

the) year. Government officials keep on warning of (a, an, the) dangers of erosion in the forests where Gujjar

herding has stripped the land. While (some, any, much) environmental groups say that these forest dwellers

have as much right to the land as the animals, other groups support the government's attempt to move the

Gujjars. The continued grazing by water buffalos risks using up the (few, less, little) food sources of elephants and other animals. Government officials plan to make (a, an) offer to the Gujjars to move them to settlements on the edge of the forests and to have them feed their animals in stalls. Park officials want to find (a, an) solution soon because they say that both the park and the Gujjars will suffer if the present situation continues.

2. Write a paragraph of your own correctly using each of the following words at least once: a, an, the, some, any, many, few, less, enough. You may want to write about how two countries vary in their concerns about wildlife.

_____

_____

_____

_____

_____

_____

_____

_____

_____

_____

_____

_____

_____

_____

_____

_____

_____

_____

_____

_____

Chapter 57 Prepositions

1. In the following paragraph, underline the correct preposition in parentheses.

       Birmingham (in, at) the spring of 1923 was a comparatively new and modern city. Lacking the Old South cultural heritage (for, of) the older southern cities such as Atlanta or Nashville, it was characterized (by, with) a tremendous energy and pursuit (on, of) success that one would expect (for, in) an emerging industrial giant. As such, it was somewhat (of, at) a melting pot (with, for) a constantly increasing number of new residents. Many were (in, from) the rural areas of the South, both black and white. There were also significant numbers of immigrants (from, in) Italy, Ireland, Germany, and the eastern European countries impoverished (by, from) war and other social and political factors. There also were smaller numbers (on, of) Asians and others. Inevitably, competition and distrust existed (with, between) these various groups, but gradually these were worked out (at, in) most cases.

2. Write sentences of your own in which you use the following prepositions.

a. on (as a preposition of time)

_____

_____

b. on (as a preposition of place)

_____

_____

c. at (as a preposition of time)

_____

_____

d. at (as a preposition of place)

_____

_____

e. in (as a preposition of time)

_____

_____

f. in (as a preposition of place)

_____

_____

g. of (to show a relationship between a part and the whole)

_____

_____

h. of (to show content)

_____

_____

i. for (to show purpose)

_____

_____

Chapter 58 Idioms

1. Write sentences of your own in which you use the following idioms.

    a. the old college try

    _____

    _____

    b. took off

    _____

    _____

    c. on the ball

    _____

    _____

    d. live high on the hog

    _____

    _____

    e. help out

    _____

    _____

    f. the bottom line

    _____

    _____

    g. come across

    _____

    _____

    h. look into (meaning to study or check on something)

    _____

    _____

i. show up

_____

_____

j. fall behind

_____

_____

Part Eight Review

ESL Concerns

Choose a paragraph of 8 to 10 sentences from a paper you have recently written or are now working on and rewrite it here, being sure that you have included all necessary subjects and verbs, that you have not repeated unnecessary words, that you have used count and noncount words correctly, that you have placed all parts of the sentence appropriately, and that you have used prepositions and idioms correctly.

PART TEN
RESEARCH

Chapter 59 Finding a Topic

59a. Deciding on a Purpose and Audience

Situation: Your American History professor has given you the following research paper assignment: "Analyze how Hollywood portrays the Vietnam War, paying special attention to the similarities and differences between three of the films you deem most representative of the genre. Imagine that your readers are generally well-educated Americans, but that they may not know specific information about the Vietnam War nor film studies."

Assignment: To help you settle on a purpose and focus your research, answer the following questions:

1. How do I figure out which movies I should use?

_____

_____

_____

_____

_____

_____

2. How can I prove what each movie's "message" is, so that I can compare their similarities and differences?

_____

_____

_____

_____

_____

_____

3. How much background information about the Vietnam War will I need to include?

_____

_____

_____

_____

_____

_____

4. How much technical information should I include about filmmaking? How should I present that technical information in the paper?

_____

_____

_____

_____

_____

_____

5. How much of my own opinion should I include in this paper?

_____

_____

_____

_____

_____

59b-e. Deciding on a Topic, Narrowing the Topic, Formulating a Research Question, and Formulating a Thesis

For each of the research paper general subjects listed below, narrow the subject into a manageable topic for a research paper which would be due two weeks from the date of the assignment. Then formulate a research question about your topic, and formulate a thesis statement that answers your research question.

EXAMPLE

Subject: World War II

Topic: How WWII brought more women into the workforce

Research Question: How did the economic demands of World War II affect women's roles in the American workforce?

Thesis Statement: Because World War II created an historic demand for manufacturing while simultaneously removing almost one-half of the men of working age, women entered the workforce to take up the slack, forever changing societal ideals of women's work.

1. Subject: college sports
   Topic:

   _____

   _____

   Research Question:

   _____

   _____

   Thesis Statement:

   _____

   _____

2. Subject: computers
   Topic:

   _____

   _____

Research Question:

_____

_____

Thesis Statement:

_____

_____

3. Subject: cultural differences
   Topic:

_____

_____

Research Question:

_____

_____

Thesis Statement:

_____

_____

4. Subject: cloning
   Topic:

_____

_____

Research Question:

_____

_____

Thesis Statement:

_____

_____

5. Subject: the media and politics
   Topic:

_____

_____

Research Question:

_____

_____

Thesis Statement:

_____

_____

Chapter 60 Searching for Information
Chapter 61 Using Web Resources

60a. Choosing Primary and Secondary Sources

Identify each of the research sources listed below as a primary or secondary source for a research paper about Ernest Hemingway.

EXAMPLE

"Hills Like White Elephants" (a short story by Hemingway)   <u>primary</u>

1. <u>The Hemingway Women</u> (a book about Hemingway)   _____

2. <u>The Sun Also Rises</u> (a novel by Hemingway)   _____

3. an encyclopedia article about Hemingway   _____

4. an informative television program about Hemingway   _____

5. <u>Hemingway on the Spanish Civil War</u> (a book of letters written by Hemingway

    and compiled by an editor)   _____

6. an Internet site about Hemingway maintained by *The New York Times*   _____

60b. Searching Libraries and Library Databases

1. Use the resources available in your college library to locate sources for a research paper on one of the other topics listed in 60a above. Using correct MLA format, list three of the sources you found. (See Chapter 66 for a complete listing of MLA formats for various types of sources.)

    Topic: _____

    Source 1:

    _____

    _____

    _____

    Source 2:

    _____

    _____

    _____

Source 3:

_____

_____

_____

2. Write a paragraph describing the process you used to find these sources.

_____

_____

_____

_____

_____

_____

_____

_____

_____

_____

_____

_____

_____

60c., 61 Searching the Internet, and Using Web Resources

1. Conduct an online search for information on one of the following topics: gender equity in college sports, the relation between video games and violence, stem-cell research, or the effects of presidential campaign debates.

   Using correct MLA format, list three sources you found that you might use for a research paper on your chosen topic.

   Topic: _____

   Source 1:

_____

_____

_____

Source 2:

_____

_____

_____

Source 3:

_____

_____

_____

2. Write a paragraph describing the process you used to find these sources.

_____

_____

_____

_____

_____

_____

_____

_____

_____

_____

_____

_____

Chapter 62 Evaluating Sources

62b. Evaluating Internet Sources

Choose one of the websites you located in the online search in the previous section of this workbook (Ch. 52b & 53). Evaluate that website using the information in Chapter 54, especially the "Checklist of questions to ask yourself about websites" on p. 348 in your handbook:

- Who is the author, organization, or sponsor? What are the credentials of this person or organization?
- What evidence is there of the accuracy of the information?
- Is the information current?
- Is there advertising on the site?
- What is the goal of the site?
- How did you access the site? Were there links from reliable sites?
- How good is the coverage of the topic?

_____

_____

_____

_____

_____

_____

_____

_____

_____

_____

_____

_____

62c-d. Evaluating Bibliographic Citations, and Evaluating Content

Examine the paragraph in the next exercise (Ch. 56) and its bibliographic citation. Evaluate the paragraph for use in an informative paper on world spices.

1. In this space, write your evaluation based on the bibliographic citation (author, timeliness, publisher/producer, audience).

_____

_____

_____

_____

_____

_____

_____

_____

_____

2. In this space, write your evaluation based on the content (accuracy, comprehensiveness, credibility, fairness, objectivity, relevance, timeliness)

_____

_____

_____

_____

_____

_____

_____

_____

_____

Chapter 64 Using Sources and Avoiding Plagiarism

64a. Understanding Why Plagiarism is Wrong

Write a paragraph explaining your understanding of
- what plagiarism is,
- what the consequences of plagiarism are in college and in the workplace,
- why plagiarism may occur,
- strategies you will employ to avoid plagiarism.

Include a description of any experience you have had or know about involving plagiarism.

_____

_____

_____

_____

_____

_____

_____

_____

_____

_____

_____

_____

_____

_____

_____

64c. Summarizing without Plagiarizing

Write a summary of the following paragraph. Assume that you read the paragraph as part of an article by Frederick Meisnier entitled "Historical Migrations of Foods," in the May 1993 issue of *International Cuisine*, pages 18-27.

One of the world's most widely used spices is the chili pepper. It gives the characteristic fire to one of India's most well-known foods, curry. In Hungary, chili pepper appears as paprika, adding a crucial bite to the flavor of goulash, and in Italy the use of chili peppers in pepperoni makes the spice a common ingredient in Italian food. The hot flavor of chilies became a staple in various foods of China, Thailand, and other Oriental countries. Five hundred years ago, however, no one in these countries had heard of the chili pepper or even had a word for it, for it was one of the treasures brought back from the New World by Christopher Columbus. When Columbus returned with his new spice, its use soon spread around the globe because it was an interesting addition to the world's spice cabinets and because it traveled well in dried form. There is even evidence of chili peppers being used as a condiment in China within a few decades after it appeared on Spanish tables. The most likely route to the Orient was by sea as the Portuguese engaged in active trading with China, particularly after the founding of their trade colony in Macao. While the Spanish were the first Europeans to encounter the New World peppers, the pepper did not become a distinctive spice in Spanish cooking. It was looked upon more as a curiosity or ornamental than as a fiery way to liven up food. Now, after centuries of use in Central and South America, the chili pepper is finally becoming more popular in North American markets through the increasing interest in Indian, Indonesian, Thai, Vietnamese, and other non-European cuisines.

Write your summary here:

_____

_____

_____

_____

_____

_____

_____

_____

64d. Paraphrasing without Plagiarizing

Paraphrase the first four sentences of the paragraph above.

_____

_____

_____

_____

_____

_____

64e-f. Using Quotation Marks to Avoid Plagiarizing, and Using Signal Words and Phrases to Integrate Sources

Follow the instructions below, using this paragraph from an article by Herbert Benson, M.D., and Julie Corliss, both of Harvard Medical School, and Geoffrey Cowley, *Newsweek*'s health editor. The article is entitled, "Brain Check," and appeared in the September 27, 2004, edition of *Newsweek* on pp. 45-47. This paragraph is on pp. 46-47.

As researchers chart the health effects of hostility and hopelessness, they're also gaining unprecedented insights into the mind's power to heal. The "placebo response" has been widely recognized since the 1950s, when Harvard's Dr. Henry Beecher described the phenomenon. Until recently, most experts dismissed it as a feat of self-deception, in which people who remain sick (or never were) convince themselves they're better. But we're now discovering that expectations can directly alter a disease process. Consider those Parkinson's sufferers who improved with sham surgery. Using PET scans, researchers compared their brains with those of patients who received an active treatment. As expected, the active intervention caused a significant rise in dopamine, the neurotransmitter that people with Parkinson's lack. But the patients who improved on placebo experienced a similar dopamine surge. A related study found that fake analgesics could boost the brain's own pain-fighting mechanisms. In both cases, the placebo response was not an imaginary lessening of symptoms but an objective, measurable change in brain chemistry.

a. Quote any complete sentence from this paragraph, introducing the quote with a partial sentence of your own that would place the sentence in the context of your paragraph. Use quotation marks and an in-text citation appropriately, and punctuate the entire sentence correctly.

_____

_____

_____

_____

b. Quote a sentence from this paragraph, leaving out several words in the middle of the sentence. Introduce the sentence appropriately, include an in-text citation, and punctuate correctly.

_____

_____

_____

c. Quote a sentence that includes a quote. Introduce the sentence appropriately, include an in-text citation, and punctuate correctly.

_____

_____

_____

_____

d. Paraphrase the last two sentences of the paragraph, quoting at least three words in sequence from one of those sentences. Introduce the sentence appropriately, include an in-text citation, and punctuate correctly.

_____

_____

_____

_____

PART ELEVEN
MLA DOCUMENTATION

Chapter 66 Documenting in MLA Style

1. Included below is a paragraph about women hikers. Following the paragraph are some sentences with information that can be added to the paragraph either as direct quotations or as information written in your own words whose source must be cited. Rewrite the paragraph so that you add at least two direct quotations and one paraphrase. Be sure to integrate the quotations and paraphrase into the paragraph, cite the sources in the paragraph, and include a list of Works Cited (in MLA format) at the end of the paragraph.

Among the other worlds of outdoor sports and recreation that women were entering before the turn of the century was hiking. Annie Smith Peck joined the list of great alpinists when she reached the peak of the Matterhorn in 1895. She was the first woman to wear pants for climbing, even though at that time women all wore floor-length skirts. Peck continued her climbing and hiking until she was seventy-five years old, including the historic first ascent of Mount Huascaran in Peru, a climb that went above 22,000 feet. In 1901, six years after Peck's assault on the Matterhorn, women joined the first Sierra Club hike. Despite Peck's famous knickerbocker pants, the Sierra Club's stated policy was that women wear skirts which could be no shorter than halfway from knee to ankle. Female hikers in great climbs became increasingly common, though not always as colorful as the famous Grandma Gatewood (Emma Gatewood), the first woman to hike the entire Appalachian Trail in one continuous stretch, in 1955. At the age of sixty-seven she hiked in sneakers and slept on a plastic shower curtain. Grandma Gatewood went on to hike the great Appalachian Trail two more times in her career.

Material to add to your version of the paragraph:

a. The historian Iris Koach, in a book entitled *Women in Sports* (published in New York in 1992 by Littleton and Crane Publishing Company), wrote the following sentence which appears on page 81:

> "Annie Smith Peck, a product of genteel Victorian wealth and exclusive private schooling, became intrigued with the idea of laying aside her scholarly efforts in order to scale the Matterhorn."

b. On page 172, Koach mentions Emma Gatewood:

> "With little publicity and less interest in commercial support for her efforts, Emma Gatewood continued to set hiking records until well into her eighties. She was an inspiration for women who saw themselves as too frail or inexperienced to hike on their own or without the support of a group of men."

c. The following sentence appears on page 45 of *Hiking American Trails* by William Byler (published in 1990 by Middlebauer Press in New York):

"By the 1950's, equipment for hiking filled specialty catalogs and took over more and more space in sporting goods stores. The selection of hiking boots, tents, backpacks, cooking utensils, and other gear had become a complicated science."

Your version of the original paragraph with the material added:

_____

_____

_____

_____

_____

_____

_____

_____

_____

_____

_____

_____

_____

_____

Your Works Cited page for your version of the paragraph you wrote in the last exercise:

_____

_____

_____

_____

_____

_____

_____

_____

2.   Listed here are a variety of sources which were used to write a paper. Using every entry listed, prepare a Works Cited page according to MLA style.

   a.   A book by Martin Joos entitled *The Five Clocks* published in New York by Harcourt, Brace, and World in 1962. The paper cited information from pages 12 and 22 of this book.

   b.   A book by Stephen Duggan and Betty Drury entitled *The Rescue of Science and Learning* published in New York by Macmillan in 1948. The paper cited information from pages 62-63.

   c.   A book entitled *Writing Centers in Context: Twelve Case Studies,* edited by Joyce A. Kinkead and Jeanette Harris and published in Urbana, Illinois, by NCTE in 1993. The paper cited information from page 74.

   d.   A poem entitled "Night Shadows" appearing in an anthology entitled *The New Gothic,* compiled and edited by Marvin Greenwood and published in New York by Chaosium in 1998. The paper cited information from page 66.

   e.   A magazine article by Robert Lillo entitled "The Electronic Industry Braces for Hard Times" appearing on pages 18-23 of the February 14, 1996, edition of *Business Weekly* magazine.

   f.   An interview with Nina Totenberg on the television program *Nightline,* produced by ABC and aired on channel WILI out of Chicago on November 23, 1995.

   g.   A citation from William Shakespeare's *Hamlet*, taken from a collection of Shakespeare's work on CD-ROM published by CMCReSearch in 1989. The CD-ROM program does not list a place of publication.

   h.   Material from an online information service, Dialog, from file 102, item 0346142. The material came from an article by Walter S. Baer entitled "Telecommunications Technology in the 1990s," published in the June 1994 edition of *Computer Science* magazine. The article began on page 152 and continued on various pages throughout the magazine.

Your Works Cited page for the sources listed in this exercise:

_____

_____

_____

_____

_____

_____

_____

_____

_____

_____

_____

_____

_____

_____

_____

3. Write an informative paragraph on chili peppers by using the information in the exercise in Chapter 56b, as well as information from **two** other sources you have found through research. Incorporate information by paraphrasing, summarizing, and quoting as appropriate from all three sources and provide parenthetical citations in MLA format. List the three sources at the end of your paragraph using MLA format for references.

Works Cited

_____

_____

_____

_____

_____

_____

_____

_____

_____

_____

_____

PART TWELVE
APA, CM, AND CSE DOCUMENTATION

Chapter 67 Documenting in APA Style

1. Included here is the same paragraph about women hikers as used in the first exercise for Chapter 58. Following the paragraph are some sentences with information that can be added to the paragraph either as direct quotations or as information written in your own words. Rewrite the paragraph so that you add at least two direct quotations and one paraphrase. Be sure to integrate the quotations and the paraphrase into the paragraph, cite the sources in the paragraph, and include a list of the works you referenced (in APA format) at the end of the paragraph.

Among the other worlds of outdoor sports and recreation that women were entering before the turn of the century was hiking. Annie Smith Peck joined the list of great alpinists when she reached the peak of the Matterhorn in 1895. She was the first woman to wear pants for climbing, even though at that time women all wore floor-length skirts. Peck continued her climbing and hiking until she was seventy-five years old, including the historic first ascent of Mount Huascaran in Peru, a climb that went above 22,000 feet. In 1901, six years after Peck's assault on the Matterhorn, women joined the first Sierra Club hike. Despite Peck's famous knickerbocker pants, the Sierra Club's stated policy was that women wear skirts which could be no shorter than halfway from knee to ankle. Female hikers in great climbs became increasingly common, though not always as colorful as the famous Grandma Gatewood (Emma Gatewood), the first woman to hike the entire Appalachian Trail in one continuous stretch, in 1955. At the age of sixty-seven she hiked in sneakers and slept on a plastic shower curtain. Grandma Gatewood went on to hike the great Appalachian Trail two more times in her career.

Material to add to your version of the paragraph:

a. The historian Iris Koach, in a book entitled *Women in Sports* (published in New York in 1992 by Littleton and Crane Publishing Company), wrote the following sentence which appears on page 81:

"Annie Smith Peck, a product of genteel Victorian wealth and exclusive private schooling, became intrigued with the idea of laying aside her scholarly efforts in order to scale the Matterhorn."

b. On page 172, Koach mentions Emma Gatewood:

"With little publicity and less interest in commercial support for her efforts, Emma Gatewood continued to set hiking records until well into her eighties. She was an inspiration for women who saw themselves as too frail or inexperienced to hike on their own or without the support of a group of men."

c. The following sentence appears on page 45 of *Hiking American Trails* by William Byler (published in 1990 by Middlebauer Press in New York):

"By the 1950's, equipment for hiking filled specialty catalogs and took over more and more space in sporting goods stores. The selection of hiking boots, tents, backpacks, cooking utensils, and other gear had become a complicated science."

Your version of the original paragraph with the material added:

_____

_____

_____

_____

_____

_____

_____

_____

_____

_____

_____

_____

_____

_____

_____

_____

_____

_____

Your References page for your version of the paragraph you wrote in the last exercise:

_____

_____

_____

_____

_____

_____

_____

_____

2. Listed here are a variety of sources which were used to write a paper. Using every entry listed, prepare a Reference page according to APA style.

    a.   A book by Martin Joos entitled *The Five Clocks* published in New York by Harcourt, Brace, and World in 1962. The paper cited information from pages 12 and 22 of this book.

    b.   A book by Stephen Duggan and Betty Drury entitled *The Rescue of Science and Learning* published in New York by Macmillan in 1948. The paper cited information from pages 62-63.

    c.   A book entitled *Writing Centers in Context: Twelve Case Studies,* edited by Joyce A. Kinkead and Jeanette Harris and published in Urbana, Illinois, by NCTE in 1993. The paper cited information from page 74.

    d.   A work entitled "Vengeance" appearing in the anthology entitled *Poetry in the Modern Age*, compiled and edited by Jason Metier and published in San Francisco by New Horizons in 1994. The paper cited information from page 54.

    e.   A magazine article by Robert Lillo entitled "The Electronic Industry Braces for Hard Times" appearing on pages 18-23 of the February 14, 1996 edition *of Business Weekly* magazine.

f. An interview with Nina Totenberg on the television program *Nightline,* produced by ABC and aired on channel WILI out of Chicago on November 23, 1995.

g. A citation from William Shakespeare's *Hamlet,* taken from a collection of Shakespeare's work on CD-ROM published by CMCReSearch in 1989. The CD-ROM program does not list a place of publication.

h. Material from an online information service, Dialog, from file 102, item 0346142. The material came from an article by Walter S. Baer entitled "Telecommunications Technology in the 1990s," published in the June 1994 edition of *Computer Science* magazine. The article began on page 152 and continued on various pages throughout the magazine.

Your Reference page for the sources listed in this exercise:

_____

_____

_____

_____

_____

_____

_____

_____

_____

_____

_____

_____

_____

_____

_____

3.   Write an informative paragraph on what studies have shown about the effect of the mind-body connection on health by using the information in the paragraph in the exercise for Chapter 56d & e, as well as information from **two** other sources you have found through research. Incorporate information by paraphrasing, summarizing, and quoting as appropriate from all three sources and provide parenthetical citations in APA format. List the three sources at the end of your paragraph using APA format for references.

_____

_____

_____

_____

_____

_____

_____

_____

_____

_____

_____

_____

_____

_____

_____

_____

References

_____

_____

_____

_____

_____

_____

_____

_____

_____

_____

_____

_____

_____

_____

_____

_____

Chapter 68 Documenting in Other Styles

Choose the letter for the preferred documentation style for source citations on teach of these topics:

Topics		**Style for Citations**
1. War-time journalism	_____	A. *Chicago Manual of Style*
2. Astronomical calculations	_____	B. *The CBE Manual* (CSE)
3. Journal of American History	_____	C. *Associated Press Style Book and Briefing on Media Law*
4. Biological control of garden pests	_____	D. *The AMS Author Handbook*
5. Geometrical theories	_____	E. *AIP Style Manual*

ANSWER KEY

Please note: Answers and sample answers cannot be provided for all exercises within this workbook. For some exercises, it is impossible to provide a sample answer which is representative of all possible correct answers. See your instructor for specific help with these exercises.

PART TWO

Chapter 1 Thinking About Writing

1a. The Rhetorical Triangle

There are many things Alan should take into consideration in tailoring his paper to the symposium; it would be impossible to list them all. Here, however, are some possible ideas:

1. An audience of concerned parents would likely be receptive to Alan's ideas. That audience, however, would be heterogeneous: people of various ethnicities, incomes, political affiliations, etc. Alan should revise his paper to make sure he is speaking to the widest audience possible, while still remaining true to the facts of the topic and his own opinion.

2. This is a new piece of evidence on the topic of child obesity that Alan can incorporate into his paper. Because it is recent and timely, it will help to establish his expertise in the subject. It might prove helpful especially in an introduction.

3. Prior to delivering his paper, Alan would be wise to find out as much as he could about this controversy, as some might take it as proof that anti-obesity initiatives may endanger children. Once he has gathered information, Alan should make sure his paper differentiates between his proposed methods and those the reality TV show employed.

4. Since Alan knows who will be challenging his ideas, he should make sure his paper preemptively addresses the issues they are likely to bring up. For instance, he might address the issue of higher taxes by arguing that preventing obesity in children will actually lower the tax burden on Americans in the long run, since more children will grow up without obesity-related health problems that, through Medicare, the government would have to pay for.

1e. Medium

1. For one example of a poster, visit http://www.spokanecitycd.org/housing/pictures/lead%20poster.jpg . Note: this poster does not fulfill the third bullet of the assignment.

2. Visit the New York State Department of Health's web site and compare your efforts to theirs: http://www.health.state.ny.us/environmental/lead/exposure/ childhood/finalplantoc.htm.

3. For a sample of the kind of tone, language and style that are appropriate for this type of letter, visit http://www.health.state.ny.us/environmental/lead/exposure/ Childhood/finalplanstate.htm.

Chapter 3 Paragraphs

3a. Unity

Responses will vary but should mention that the sentence about the weather in Tibet should be deleted for the sake of unity.

3b. Coherence

Responses will vary but should mention that although the paragraph is well written, it would benefit from added transition between sentences.

3c. Development

Responses will vary but should mention that the paragraph lacks adequate development.

Chapter 4 Argument

4e. Logical Fallacies.

1. Bandwagon
2. Hasty Generalization
3. Either ... Or
4. False Analogy
5. Personal Attack
6. No fallacy
7. Doubtful Cause
8. Irrelevant Proof
9. Hasty generalization
10. Begging the question

Chapter 6 Document Design

6a. Principles of Document Design

The restaurant guide lists ethnic restaurants two ways:

1.   By ethnicity

   • Chinese restaurants

   • Italian restaurants

   • Mexican restaurants

2.   By neighborhood

6c. Paper Preparation

1. APA

2. MLA

3. APA

4. APA

5. MLA

6. APA

7. MLA

6d. Multimedia Presentations

For this exercise, answers will (and should!) vary greatly. There are, however, several things to keep in mind when evaluating this assignment:

- Does the presentation maintain the dignity and solemnity of the occasion?
- Does the presentation effectively make use of image and sound? While neither is necessarily required, both can greatly enhance a presentation.
- Does the presentation distract the audience from the speaker?
- Is the presentation entertaining? Does it effectively teach a modern audience about the Gettysburg Address?
- Does the presentation give anything for the audience to take away with them (e.g. handouts) at the end?

6e. Web Page Design

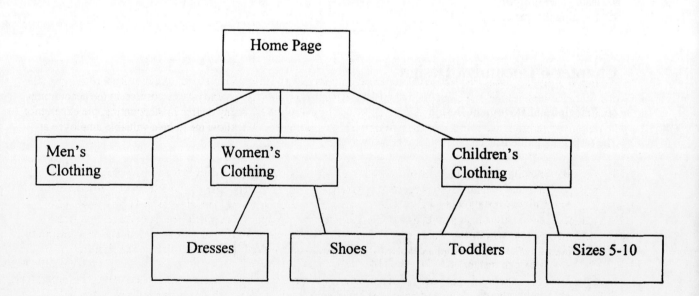

PART THREE
COMMON CATEGORIES OF WRITING

Chapter 7 Writing about Literature

7c. Conventions in Writing about Literature

1.   past tense

2.   present tense

3.   present tense

4.   past tense

Chapter 8 Professional Writing

8d. Cover Letters

The letter might be rewritten in a number of ways. Below is one model.

222 Lanbow Road
Seabrook, NH 03874
May 24, 2008

Mr. Donald Wasserman
LPIN Financial
224 Eden Avenue, Suite 7S
Washington, DC 20055

Dear Mr. Wasserman:

We met at a job fair sponsored by the Career Development Center at the University of New Hampshire in April of this year, and at that time you mentioned that LPIN Financial would have an entry-level position in the accounting department available beginning in June. I am applying for that position, as my degree in Accounting, the experience I have gained through two accounting internships, and my work ethic will allow me to be a valuable employee at LPIN Financial.

I have graduated summa cum laude from the University of New Hampshire with a B.B.A. in Accounting. It is a rigorous program that specializes in preparing its graduates to work in corporate accounting. As my résumé will attest, I have also served as an intern at two different companies: Tunrow and Gaddis, a well-known financial services company in New Hampshire, and at Curtis Richards, a company that specializes in personal and small business income tax preparation. Furthermore, I served as treasurer of both the Accounting Club and the University of New Hampshire's Phi Beta Kappa chapter, which helped about record keeping and money management.

I am available for an interview at your convenience and am more than happy to meet with you in your Washington office. I will telephone in ten days to finalize our arrangements and to learn whether you need any additional information. If you prefer, please feel free to call me at (603) 555-4892 or to e-mail me at georgelogan@unh.edu.

Thank you for considering my application. I look forward to meeting with you in the near future.

Sincerely,

George Logan

Enclosure: Résumé

PART FOUR
REVISING SENTENCES

Chapter 10 Comma Splices and Fused Sentences

Responses will vary, but one possible revision is provided here.

Our country seems to be going through a change in attitudes. Unlike our forefathers, we Americans are now encouraged to get as much as possible as quickly as possible. This attitude is expressed on television; advertising also plays on this appeal. Many see a relationship between these current attitudes and gambling on lotteries. It is easy to understand why more and more people are handing their money over to chance, fate, and luck if what they are looking for is instant gratification. Statistics show this attitude is growing: in the late 80s, state lotteries grew an average of 17.5 percent annually—roughly as fast as the computer industry. High-tech advertising for the lotteries takes attention away from the fact that a player has virtually no chance of winning. Advertisements focus instead on the fantasy of what it would be like to win. Surveys conducted by state lotteries show that few players have a clear understanding of how dismal their odds of winning really are. A player has a better chance of being struck by lightning than of winning a lottery.

Chapter 11 Subject-Verb Agreement

1.   is

        weighs

        finds

        sell

        is

        want

        depends

        is

        strike

        do

        are

        are

        is

2. Sentences will vary but the verb forms should be as follows:

a. Singular

b. Plural

c. Plural

d. Plural

e. Plural

f. Plural

g. Singular

h. Singular

i. Singular

j. Plural

k. Singular

l. Singular or plural depending upon how committee is used

m. Singular

n. Plural

o. Singular

p. Singular

q. Plural

r. Singular

s. Plural

t. Singular

u. Plural

v. Singular

w. Plural

Chapter 12 Sentence Fragments

1. complete sentence

2. complete sentence

3. fragment

4. complete sentence

5. fragment

6. complete sentence

7. fragment

8. complete sentence

9. fragment

10. fragment

11. fragment

12. complete sentence

Chapter 13 Dangling and Misplaced Modifiers

13a. Dangling Modifiers

The great memorials in the nation's capital are slowly deteriorating. Having faced the elements for seven decades, even casual tourists can see that the Lincoln Memorial is wearing down. Water is causing the steel structures embedded in the concrete slabs to deteriorate. At the Jefferson Memorial, which is built on clay fill, the steps are starting to pull away from the base of the monument, and there are cracks appearing in the dome. Being washed daily, details in the marble carvings of both monuments are falling off. Air pollution and acid rain are also contributing to the gradual disintegration. To find a solution, constant studies by the National Park Service are being conducted, but the caretakers of the monuments are pessimistic. Exposure to the elements, they say, causes some deterioration that cannot be stopped. <u>Looking more like ruins than buildings</u>, it is hard to watch these noble monuments wear away.

13b. Misplaced Modifiers

The Food and Drug Administration (FDA) claims that it has found tiny amounts of drug residue in milk samples <u>in a report issued recently</u>. The level of contamination is so low that there is no real safety problem in the nation's milk supply, but a ban has been put on one drug, sulfamethazine, found in a few samples, to prohibit its use with beef cattle and pigs <u>by farmers</u>. The FDA has already banned the use of sulfamethazine with milk cows. However, there is still concern that some dairy farmers or veterinarians use the drug improperly <u>among members of Congress</u>, even though recent testing of milk samples only found a few traces of sulfa drugs <u>in a large number</u>. The FDA is now calling on dairy farmers and veterinarians to eliminate all illegal uses of veterinary drug products. Farmers are already <u>almost all</u> complying with this order.

Additional Modifier Exercises

Responses will vary, but possible revisions are provided here.

1. Scientists have discovered Cro-Magnon man was human because he used primitive tools.

2. Using a large flashlight, Bob stunned the pit bull.

3. As we walked into the house's entryway, the lamp glowed warmly.

4. Mark on the enclosed card which magazine you choose.

5. Sue found a woman's emerald bracelet.

6. As one approaches the city from the west, the sports arena is quite a sight.

Chapter 14 Parallel Constructions

Recently, two pilots, <u>one in a 175-seat commercial airliner</u> and <u>the other one in a small, twin-engine corporate jet</u>, were barreling toward each other. On the instrument panel of the commercial jet, <u>a small air traffic screen flashed a yellow circle</u> and <u>a voice announced, "Traffic."</u> As the yellow circle approached the center of the screen, it changed to a red square. The voice said loudly, "Climb, <u>climb."</u> <u>As he noticed the red square</u> and <u>as he pulled up</u>, the pilot saw the other craft fly past several hundred feet below. The voice that called out the warning was <u>not the copilot</u> but <u>the latest audiovisual aid to arrive in cockpits of planes</u>, a traffic alert and collision avoidance system. The Federal Aviation Administration has issued an order <u>that this system must be installed in 20 percent of all large commercial planes by next year</u> and <u>that this system must be installed in 20 percent of all large commercial planes using American airspace within the next three years</u>. The system works by <u>computing the distance between planes</u>, <u>warning planes when they get within six miles of each other</u>, and then deciding which plane should climb and which should descend to avoid a collision.

Chapter 15 Consistency (Avoiding Shifts)

Responses will vary, but one possible revision is provided here.

High school proms used to be dances where students dressed up in suits and dresses and celebrated their coming graduation, but now they have to spend a lot of money for a tuxedo or elegant formal dress. Proms have become big business as formalwear shops and limousine services offer their services in advertising campaigns. Tuxedo rental shops across the country report that proms, not weddings, account for the major proportion of their businesses. The typical expenses now include the tuxedo rental, prom tickets, corsage, dinner, and limousine rental. High-school graduates can easily spend $300 on the dance, and that may be just for the basics. Prom-goers can spend additional funds for the latest fashions in tuxes, and they can buy photos for $50 or more. Even when the prom is over, there are other expenses. Some graduates go away for the whole weekend, often to a resort hotel. So there are additional costs for a hotel, and if parents are along as chaperones, it is necessary to add in the cost of their rooms and meals, too. High-school graduates insist that this is all necessary as a rite of passage, but parents who often have to contribute at least part of the funds do not appreciate the expense.

Chapter 16 Faulty Predication

With the present concern for the environment, some companies are trying to increase their sales by advertising their products as environmentally safe. The makers of some plastic trash bags, for example, are claiming that their plastic is degradable. The reason for the claim is that there are additives that cause the product to break down after prolonged exposure to sunlight. Biodegradability, they assert, occurs when there is photodegradability, a breakdown by sunlight. But since most trash bags are buried in landfills, the benefits of photodegradability are questionable. Thus, the government has stated that one way to improve deceptive advertising claims is to eliminate false or misleading information.

Chapter 17 Coordination and Subordination

Responses will vary, but one possible revision is provided here.

Americans have become videotape addicts. Because over 75 percent of all American households now have videocassette recorders, hotels hope to make their guests feel at home by providing equipment for watching videotapes. Some of the largest hotel chains in the country have added videocassette recorders in the rooms which can be used by renting videocassettes from shops in the hotel. In these shops, which have a good selection of recent movies for guests to view in their rooms, hotels guests can show their room key and can rent a movie at a reasonable rate. Other hotels don't want to bother with stores in the lobby, and they are exploring a different option. They are adding automated video dispensing machines in their lobbies that hold hundreds of titles and have new releases as well as standard favorites. One hotel chain, which has a lot of large business conventions, has investigated another approach. It is offering to distribute to guests videotapes that the corporation holding the convention wants its participants to see. Corporations like this because the videotapes can convey some of the key ideas being presented at the convention. Videotape players in hotel rooms may soon be standard equipment, just as television sets were added years ago. When Americans became addicted to television, they expected to watch television in their hotel rooms.

Chapter 18 Sentence Clarity

Responses will vary, but one possible revision is provided here.

A new approach to using computers may be to jot handwritten notes onto an electronic pad. This is done by a special pen that projects a narrow light beam onto the pad. For computer users who have had to rely on entering data into a computer by means of a keyboard, it is a major step forward in using computers. Typing is more distracting than writing for many people who are not skilled typists but who use computers frequently. For the last twenty-five years, the goal of computer developers has been to rid the computer of keyboards, but more development in the field of character recognition is needed. One way to eliminate the keyboard is to teach computers to read through optical character recognition. Another way is to recognize the human voice instead of typed data. But speech recognition is not advancing as rapidly as some computer developers would like. It is not likely that the near future will see computers we can converse with because we have no appropriate technology that is this advanced. More promising is the ability of the computer to scan images. Already character recognition machines scan pages of printed material. Computer developers are also considering electronic gloves that could be used by people to point to areas of the screen. There is no limit to what will be coming next in computer development. The result of doing away with the keyboard will be to save time and to eliminate all those typos.

Chapter 19 Transitions

Responses will vary, but one possible revision is provided here.

My father really needs help because he is a workaholic. He works nearly twelve hours a day. Doctors have told him it is not only bad for his health, but it is affecting his family, and he has worried my family to no end. My family has tried to help him, but he has not acknowledged the problem. He has a tolerance that goes through the roof. He sneaks out of the house before anyone is awake, and he gets home after most of us have finished dinner and are getting ready for bed. He works at home as well: his computer is connected to the one at his office, and his work calls him at home. He has a pager and a cell phone. Things may be getting worse since Dad accepted a promotion to regional director.

Chapter 20 Sentence Variety

1. Responses will vary, but one possible revision is provided here.

Animal rights activists, who are known primarily for their campaigns against fur coats and the use of animals in laboratories, are also campaigning against rodeos. In their public statements seeking support, protesters say that rodeo animals are being mistreated. For example, they say the animals are starving and live a life filled with pain and suffering. Although animal rights activists also say that rodeo horses buck because they are in pain, rodeo and circus owners say that this is not so. Well-fed and comfortable, these animals would be going to slaughter if they were not used as show animals. Moreover, to emphasize their point, handlers explain that they have a healthy respect for the size and power of these animals. Treated like star athletes, the animals enjoy performing. On the other hand, animal rights activists point to the use of cattle prods and bucking straps to get the animals moving, but rodeo owners argue that even ranchers have to use electric prods to get herds moving. Before prods were used, ranchers used pitchforks. Calf roping, also condemned by animal rights activists, can break calves' necks and can also snap vertebrae and legs. Calf roping, to the satisfaction of animal rights activists, has been banned in some states. Eliminating calf roping, they hope, can result in the overall elimination of rodeo shows. However, rodeo owners protest that breaking of calves' necks, bones, and vertebrae just doesn't happen, and they invite activists to come to rodeos and see for themselves.

3. Responses will vary, but one possible revision is provided here.

Gardening can be a worthwhile activity because the gardener can produce food for her family, as well as helping to save the environment and prevent the overuse of landfills. One way to do this is by mulching, which is actually recycling. The gardener can recycle clippings when she mows the lawn in the summer and leaves when she rakes in the fall, along with scraps from the kitchen all year long. Usually the clippings, leaves, and scraps are gathered in large plastic bags and taken to the landfills. To use these items as organic mulch, the gardener should collect them in a corner of the garden and mix them all together. Later, she can spread the mulch on the garden to provide nutrients which will cause the soil to produce bigger and better vegetables, thus providing her with many benefits.

PART FIVE
PARTS OF SENTENCES

Chapter 21 Verbs

21a. Verb Phrases

Some scientists <u>are saying</u> that a buildup of carbon dioxide and other greenhouse gases in the atmosphere <u>will cause</u> global warming. But another group of scientists <u>argue</u> that we <u>should study</u> the data more carefully before any firm conclusions <u>are drawn</u>. While scientists generally <u>agree</u> that an unchecked accumulation of greenhouse gases <u>will cause</u> changes, no one <u>knows</u> when it <u>will start</u>, how much <u>will happen</u>, or how rapidly it <u>will occur</u>. The most widely accepted estimate is that there <u>will be</u> a rise in the earth's average temperature as early as 2050. This <u>could bring</u> rising sea levels and severe droughts in some areas. But no one <u>knows</u> yet how clouds and the ocean's ability to absorb heat <u>will affect</u> this. When scientists <u>understand</u> this better, projections <u>can be revised</u>.

21b. Verb Forms

The evidence that global <u>warming</u> has <u>started</u> is not very strong. Some scientists believe that the concentration of carbon dioxide has <u>increased</u> over 25 percent since the early 1800s, but other scientists point to the fact that the average global temperature has <u>risen</u> by no more than a half degree Centigrade. Even that rise is questionable since there was a <u>cooling</u> period from 1940 to 1970 that caused forecasters <u>to predict</u> a return to the ice ages. Therefore, <u>to act</u> on predictions by <u>passing</u> laws that restrict or ban the use of fossil fuels may be hasty, but <u>conserving</u> energy, <u>banning</u> harmful chlorofluorocarbons, and <u>planting</u> more trees <u>to absorb</u> carbon dioxide from the air seems sensible. Many industries are also <u>acting</u> more responsibly and are <u>reducing</u> hazardous emissions from their factories.

21c. Verb Tense

1.   In 1987, the FBI (<u>opened</u>, has opened, was opening) a $1.5 million mock-up of a small town in Virginia named Hogan's Alley. Presently, the town's population (has been, will be, <u>is</u>) about 200. Generally, Hogan's Alley (has looked, <u>looks</u>, is looking) like any peaceful little American town, but often the quiet (will be shattered, <u>is shattered</u>, had been shattered) by the sound of a shotgun or squealing tires. Then prospective G-men who (<u>had been sitting</u>, sat, will sit) outside the post office jump in their cars and race after the "criminals." None of this (will be, <u>is</u>, is being) real because Hogan's Alley (<u>is</u>, has been, had been) a training academy for those who (will want, <u>want</u>, will have wanted) to become FBI agents. Next year over 500 trainees (will have attended, attend, <u>will attend</u>) classes in frisking, lectures on handcuffing, and seminars on interrogating witnesses. The FBI (<u>started</u>, was starting, had started) Hogan's Alley because it wanted its agents to have more true-to-life experience before they go out and deal with dangerous criminals. So now every day there (will be, have been, <u>are</u>) mock bank robberies, kidnappings, and drug busts. The "criminals," however, are actors, part-time students, retirees, off-duty policemen and firemen, and anyone else who (<u>has passed</u>, will pass, had passed) the rigorous screening tests.

2.   Last year, in Hogan's Alley, the FBI's mock-up village for prospective FBI agents, the trainees <u>took</u> part in an intensive 14-week training course. About 46 agents <u>moved</u> through the program which <u>began</u> with lessons in surveillance. Trainees <u>tracked</u> a suspect from his home as he <u>drove</u> to a shopping mall and <u>sold</u> a small bag of phony cocaine. Next <u>came</u> a class in simple arrests, when agents-in-training <u>burst</u> into a fleabag motel and <u>took</u> an unarmed burglar as he <u>lay</u> in bed. Agents <u>learned</u> how to frisk suspects, and then they <u>read</u> them their rights. Instructors, who <u>brought</u> their own experience as former FBI agents to the teaching, carefully <u>gave</u> advice to each trainee and <u>provided</u> pointers on how to handle details such as slipping on handcuffs during a struggle. Nine weeks into the course, trainees <u>got</u> some practice in arresting an armed felon. Their final lessons <u>took</u> place in a courtroom, where they <u>faced</u> a team of actors who <u>posed</u> as a tough team of defense lawyers. Those trainees who <u>did</u> not flunk out of the course <u>became</u> FBI agents, and the actors, who <u>played</u> drug peddlers, burglars, and other felons, <u>said</u> that seeing what it is like being on the wrong end of the law <u>reminded</u> them that they <u>did</u> not want to become criminals themselves.

21d. Verb Voice

Like many cities built on a river, Kansas City is divided (<u>passive</u>) between two states. The biggest single municipality is Kansas City, Missouri, but over one-half of the population of the metropolitan area lives (<u>active</u>) in various suburban cities on the Kansas side. Problems are created (<u>passive</u>) when it comes time to finance projects that will benefit (<u>active</u>) both sides of the state line. In the 1990s, cities on both sides of the state line agreed (<u>active</u>) to a bi-state sales tax to be used to renovate Kansas City, Missouri's Union Station. Advocates said (<u>active</u>) the new station would bring (<u>active</u>) in tourism that would benefit both sides of the state line. Opponents claimed (<u>active</u>) Kansas City, Missouri was just trying to dip (<u>active</u>) into the pockets of the more affluent suburbs on the Kansas side. In the end, a compromise was reached (<u>passive</u>). The bi-state sales tax was passed (<u>passive</u>), but all contributing cities had (<u>active</u>) a say in its use and the tax had (<u>active</u>) a 5-year duration. It was not renewed (<u>passive</u>).

21e. Verb Mood

Singles bars and dating services are thriving (<u>declarative</u>), but there are always new approaches. In commercial dating services, one new approach that may be cheaper (<u>subjunctive</u>) than the standard videotaped interviews is the lunch-date service. For less than $50 a month, the company promises (<u>declarative</u>) three lunch dates a month. People are paired on the basis of simple criteria gathered from brief interviews that might last (<u>subjunctive</u>) less than five minutes. The company sets up the lunch date, and the participants take it from there. "Meet (<u>imperative</u>) new people," says the advertising brochure, "and enjoy (<u>imperative</u>) some interesting little restaurants." Since the Census Bureau puts (<u>declarative</u>) the number of single adults at 66 million and growing, these new twists on dating services may prosper (<u>subjunctive</u>).

21f. Modal Verbs

When American products began appearing in Moscow, city officials worried that the signs and advertising for these products <u>might</u> make (<u>could possibly make</u>) Moscow look less Russian. A law recently passed in Moscow warns that all stores and businesses <u>must</u> display (<u>need to display</u>) signs in Russian or at least change them into the Cyrillic alphabet. This has caused many businesses to contact the city inspector because of questions they have. For example, one businessman wondered whether he <u>should</u> change (<u>is obliged to change</u>) the letters in the label for the Puma running shoes that he sells. He was concerned that changing the letters from English to Russian <u>might</u> make (<u>has the possibility of making</u>) the shoes less well-known. The problem became confusing because the new law does not forbid foreign words but does require the Russian sign to be bigger than the one in English. Different stores found different solutions. An American cosmetics company, Estee Lauder, announced that they <u>will</u> put (<u>strongly intend to put</u>) one sign with the Russian alphabet on their awning and another sign with the English alphabet in the windows. Despite all the questions and worries, the inspector in charge of enforcing this rule will be very strict about checking on foreign signs.

Chapter 22 Nouns and Pronouns

22a. Nouns

Sports fanatics are spending large sums of money these <u>days</u> to purchase sports memorabilia. In fact, says one of the <u>industry's spokespersons</u>, it is a $100 million-a-year obsession. Buyers look for scorecards, stadium seats, autographed baseball bats, and even <u>children's</u> clothing that belonged to old-time greats such as Babe Ruth. <u>Ruth's</u> personal letter to a fan recently sold for over $7000. Since Joe Lewis, the famous boxer, kept many of his old <u>mouthpieces, collectors</u> are paying over $2000 for boxed sets of Lewis's mouthpieces. There is even a magazine entitled *Sports Collectors Digest* which keeps <u>collectors</u> informed about many of the <u>auctions</u> and the availability of various <u>items</u> of interest. A faculty member in the history department of a major American university has begun a study of this phenomenon and reports that yearly increases in prices are staggering. For example, he says, a nineteenth-century baseball card of an obscure Hall of Fame pitcher, Tim O'Keefe, which was worth about $750 two <u>years</u> ago, recently sold for over $30,000. <u>O'Keefe's</u> other memorabilia are expected to soar in value as well. Sports <u>collectibles</u> are now big business.

22b. Pronouns

The business of sports collectibles has become so profitable that <u>it</u> has attracted con artists <u>who</u> manage to forge and sell bogus items. The forgeries have become such big business, in fact, that many con artists help <u>one another</u> and have developed a large network of bogus items. <u>These</u> items include fake Joe DiMaggio signatures and imitation press box pins. <u>Anyone who</u> is in the memorabilia business can spot <u>these</u> forgeries and fakes, but sports fans are often too enthusiastic about a purchase to take the time to have <u>their</u> purchases checked by experts. As a result, <u>they</u> often allow <u>themselves</u> to be conned. A lot of junk from people's attics is also cluttering the market. When <u>someone</u> finds yellowed pages from 1929 sports sections in <u>her</u> scrapbook, <u>she</u> may think <u>she</u> has an expensive treasure. Flea markets overflow with <u>these</u> antiques <u>which</u> may or may not be worth anything. But if a buyer is willing to pay large sums of money, <u>who</u> can say whether <u>that</u> autographed photo or threadbare jersey is or is not a treasure worth collecting? With a market <u>where</u> buyers pay $20,000 for <u>one</u> of Lou Gehrig's old bats, <u>it</u> is worth cleaning out <u>those</u> old attics and scrapbooks.

Chapter 23 Pronoun Case and Reference

23a. Pronoun Case

1.   When historian Page Smith began to ask himself just what kind of education was being provided by American universities, he started with a list of questions. <u>His</u> answers can be found in his book entitled *Killing the Spirit*. <u>Those</u> readers looking for encouraging conclusions will not find <u>them</u> in this report as Smith criticizes professors' lack of interest in teaching and <u>their</u> tendency to spend too much time writing books and articles that do not contribute anything useful to mankind's betterment. Smith finds <u>those</u> academics who look down on teaching as less important than research to be at fault. For <u>him</u>, the student revolt of the 1960s and early 1970s was a time when students were looking for answers to important questions but got no help from their professors. There was no dialogue between their professors and <u>them</u> that addressed questions about meaning and values in life, says Smith. However, community colleges and small, independent colleges still concern <u>themselves</u> with the needs of students. University administrators <u>who</u> are more interested in budgets and specific agendas will not find answers in Smith's book, and readers will wonder who his real audience is. To <u>whom</u> should <u>we</u> look for answers?

3.   Fall break was over, and the research assignment was due the next day, so Ross asked Lucy if she wanted to go to the library with Amy and him. The instructor had told the class that the students who made high grades on the midterm exam would be those who had read the assignments and completed all the homework. When the girls and he reached the reference room, they saw several classmates whom they could work with. They asked their friends, "Who has finished the assignment?" They were surprised that all the other students were finished and headed to Starbucks. It was clear that a long night lay ahead for the girls and him. The next day, Ross asked the teacher, "Please give Lucy, Amy, and me one more day to finish the research assignment." But the teacher said that wouldn't be fair to the rest of the students who had all worked hard, so Ross and they learned, yet again, not to procrastinate.

23b. Pronoun Reference

When Benjamin Franklin discovered electricity in thunderclouds, he sparked a controversy that still has no clear answer. How do clouds become electrified in the first place? To this day <u>they</u> haven't been able to adequately explain how <u>it</u> contains such incredible amounts of electricity that a stroke of lightning can contain about 100 million volts. One researcher who wants to find some answers flies his plane into storms to measure electric fields and ice particle changes. It's bumpy work, he says, especially if there are large hailstones because <u>it</u> can damage the plane and the measuring equipment. On one trip <u>they</u> noticed that in sections of clouds where water and ice mix, the measuring devices picked up indications of strong charge separation. The answer may be that in a certain temperature range, the temperature can cause the charge separation. Another factor may be a kind of soft hail called "graupel," pea-sized particles that can look like miniature raspberries. They form when droplets of supercooled water collide, freezing together instantly. Ice crystals then bounce off the growing graupel, building up a charge from the friction just as you build up a static electricity charge when you scuff your feet across the carpet. When they are carried to different parts of the cloud, the result is a separation of the positively and negatively charged particles. Then, when the electrical difference between the ground and the sky becomes great enough, everyone should haul his or her kite in.

Chapter 24 Adjective and Adverbs

24a. Adjectives and Adverbs

For many people, the crossword puzzle in the daily paper is one of life's little pleasures. Some say it is also surely one of life's frustrations. While puzzle books conveniently include the answers in the back, most newspapers print the answers the next day. Now there is a quicker answer. Some companies have an automated solution. Readers can dial an 800 service for instant answers. This service is free to callers but is paid for by advertisers who sponsor each day's puzzle. An advertiser can run a small advertisement by the puzzle and can include a ten-second message that callers will hear before the answers are given. The New York Times handles this differently. For their puzzles, callers pay for all requests for clues. These services are a major breakthrough for frustrated puzzle-doers who are used to waiting until the next day.

24b. A, An, The

After winding down twenty miles of dirt road in Mtunthama, Malawi, (no article) visitors will come upon the well-kept lawns and gardens of (the) Kamuzu Academy, one of (no article) Africa's most unusual schools. Here, on four hundred acres of well-trimmed lands is (a) school dedicated to classical scholarship. (The) school was founded by President Hastings Kamuzu Banda, the ruler of Malawi since it won its independence from (the) British in 1964. Originally, Dr. Banda studied at (a) Scottish missionary school in Malawi and went on to study in (no article) South Africa, (the) United States of America, and (no article) Britain, where he acquired (a) medical degree and (a) love of Latin and Greek, as well as a strong attraction to the classical emphasis of the elite British schools. When Dr. Banda returned to Malawi, he wanted to copy (the) architecture and curriculum of Eton and other British boarding schools. Some critics in opposition to Dr. Banda say that (the) academy is not appropriate in their country where ordinary schools often do not have (no article) textbooks and where more than two-thirds of (the) population are illiterate. However, defenders of the school point out that the school is not elite in choosing its students. Children are accepted without regard to their family's wealth or position. Each year 35,000 students take (an) exam to try to gain entrance to the school which accepts about eighty new students (a) year. Once accepted, all students are required to take four years of (no article) Latin and four years of (no article) ancient Greek, along with (no article) English, (no article) mathematics, and (a) history course about Africa. Most graduates go on to university and then take jobs in (the) Malawi civil service.

24c. Comparisons

1. larger

2. largest

3. more exciting

4. most enjoyable

5. user-friendliest (or most user-friendly)

6. better

7. best

8. worst

Chapter 25 Prepositions

Americans used to pour ketchup over so many foods that it was America's favorite condiment. Now salsa has replaced ketchup as the favorite <u>between</u> the two <u>in</u> American food markets. Salsa, which means "sauce" <u>in</u> Spanish, is defined as any fresh-tasting, chunky mixture, usually made with tomatoes, chilies, onions, and other seasonings. Although salsa used to be associated <u>with</u> Mexican and southwestern cooking, it is being used for a variety of foods not particularly Mexican. The popularity <u>of</u> salsa is apparently part of the current food trend as Americans become more interested <u>in</u> spicier foods. In 1988, only 16 percent of households <u>in</u> America bought salsa. <u>In</u> two years, that figure was up to 36 percent, and the market continues to grow <u>at</u> a very fast rate. A marketing information company notes that salsas and picante—which are different <u>from</u> salsas because they are thinner—account <u>for</u> about two-thirds of this market, a category that also includes taco and enchilada sauces. As the market expands, so do the choices. The simplest salsas are based <u>on</u> chopped tomatoes and chilies, and the types of chilies determine how hot the particular type of salsa is. Cookbooks with a variety of recipes indicate the preference of some people to make their salsas <u>at</u> home. Salsas are one of the few popular snack foods that are fat-free or nearly so, and many are made without preservatives, two characteristics that may contribute <u>to</u> their popularity now that people are interested <u>in</u> eating healthier. Riding on this wave of popularity are the new fruit salsas, made with peaches, pineapples, and so on, and vegetable salsas, made with pinto beans, corn, and black-eyed peas. Other varieties will surely appear as the market expands <u>in</u> the future.

Chapter 26 Subjects

Because television <u>viewers</u> of sporting events like to follow the actions of specific players, a cable <u>company</u> in New York is trying out a new subscription service. If <u>it</u> is successful, <u>it</u> is likely to become available to everyone. Cable <u>subscribers</u> will be able to tune into a tournament and pick the player <u>they</u> want to follow. Using a wand similar to a TV remote control, <u>viewers</u> sitting at home will be able to switch from conventional network coverage to a camera <u>that</u> focuses solely on the preferred player. Instant <u>replays</u> and a <u>list</u> of statistics on selected pros will be other selections that the <u>service</u> will provide. This interactive <u>technology</u> will allow viewers to customize programming. While the present <u>programming</u> is only a test of the technology, some cable <u>companies</u> foresee customers being able to sign up for interactive television just like other cable services. When will this <u>service</u> be available for everyone? It is too soon to know for sure, but there is certainly a large <u>demand</u> for such services.

Chapter 27 Phrases

1. c
2. b
3. f
4. c

5. e
6. a
7. d

Chapter 28 Clauses

28a. Independent Clauses

If you are a magician and like highly structured organizations, <u>you may want to join either the International Brotherhood of Magicians or the Society of American Magicians</u>. If, however, you are a magician who lives in New York City and likes to gather informally with other magicians, <u>you should visit Reuben's Restaurant on 38th Street</u>

and Madison Avenue any Saturday afternoon. There will be professional and amateur magicians sitting in the back room, and they will be swapping tricks or polishing their routines on each other. People come in with jumbo interlocking rings, decks of cards, and brightly colored scarves in their pockets. Some are doctors, professors, salespersons in shoe stores, tax attorneys, shipping clerks, or teenagers who are just learning the basics. Others are professionals who have appeared on *The Tonight Show* or in traveling circuses. They all share a love of magic, and they willingly sit and watch each other's routines because they know how valuable it is to keep practicing.

28b. Dependent Clauses

There are an estimated 50,000 magicians in America. Most are amateurs who enjoy magic as a hobby. These amateurs often have elaborate equipment although their only audience is usually their friends and relatives. Some, however, specialize in the small card, coin, and rope tricks that are always popular. Purists call this intimate "close-up" magic the only real magic because it relies so heavily on a person's manual dexterity. Because people seem to prefer to be fooled face-to-face, this close-up magic is also offered by professional magicians who perform at birthday parties and trade shows. A psychologist who is also a magician says that when something is done under people's noses, it's more magical. It's much more elusive. The spectacular effects of magic done on television don't seem to impress people quite so much. Whatever the cause may be, amateur magicians will keep buying those sponge balls, decks of cards, special coins, and paper flowers.

Chapter 29 Essential and Nonessential Clauses and Phrases

Responses will vary, but one possible revision is provided here.

Music teachers in the elementary schools who want to teach classical music to their students now have a lot of materials to help them. The materials have been developed by a group of educators who want to introduce classical music appreciation programs in elementary schools. Many students say these materials are excellent. These programs are also being used to coach students for contests. The programs incorporate listening skills and information about themes, styles, and forms of music. Students seem to enjoy these contests. The contests are a new form of competition in many schools. Contestants are often asked to identify the main themes of familiar works such as *Nutcracker Suite,* the specific instruments being played, and the composers. Harder questions are those that are asked about music the students have not studied in school. These questions stump even the more experienced teams. Not all the music that is studied in the music appreciation classes is classical. Sometimes jazz and non-Western music is added, though students also seem to enjoy studying classical music that they have heard on television commercials. Music teachers who have tried these programs are pleased with the variety of types of music students come to like and the quantity of music they come to know. These music appreciation programs are expanding rapidly across the nation. The programs were begun on a small scale in a few states.

Chapter 30 Sentences

1. c
2. c
3. e
4. b
5. e
6. c

7. a
8. a
9. e
10. d
11. c

PART SIX
STYLE AND WORD CHOICE

Chapter 32 General and Specific Language

32a. General Versus Specific Statements

Answers will vary. A successful final sentence for each of the three prompts will incorporate much, if not all, of the information generated from the preceding questions. Furthermore, each sentence, while being long, will be grammatically correct.

32b. General Versus Specific Words

Responses will vary, but one possible revision is provided here.

People like driving up for fast food, and now so do their <u>spaniels and collies</u>. A new fast-food industry has begun for drive-in dog food, and the menu is entirely for <u>dogs</u>. These new <u>businesses</u> offer treats to dogs with dog biscuits shaped to resemble <u>the kind of fast food people have</u>. The dog biscuits are made from <u>foods </u>that help keep dogs healthy. The biscuits are <u>flavored differently</u> so that dogs don't get tired of the same thing. Customers love the idea of <u>going to</u> a doggy drive-in after picking up their own <u>fast food</u>. So far the menu has been limited to dog biscuits, but <u>some people</u> will come up with new ideas for better <u>food products</u> for dogs.

32c. Concrete Versus Abstract Words

Responses will vary, but one possible revision is provided here.

When hikers reach a stream, they often decide to cross where the <u>dirt trail slopes down to</u> the water. But this may not be the best place at which to cross. Water usually moves most swiftly at the narrowest part of the stream. So, hikers should instead look for another spot where the stream widens. Here the current often <u>slows</u> <u>down</u> and may be easier to walk through. When hikers are carrying a backpack, they should loosen the shoulder straps and hip belt before <u>wading in</u> so that they can toss off the pack <u>if they stumble or lose their balance</u>. Some hikers find that if they suddenly hit a depression in the streambed, the weight of the backpack can toss them off balance. Another aid to crossing a stream is a good hiking stick. It can serve as another leg, offering better balance when there are <u>slippery rocks underfoot</u>. It is helpful to remove unneeded <u>sweaters, heavy pants, or boots</u> before crossing a stream with a swift current because the water can drag against <u>waterlogged vests and jeans</u>. The hiker should also take each step slowly and deliberately. The forward foot should be planted firmly before the rear foot is moved. Finally, the careful hiker never hurries across a stream.

Chapter 33 Conciseness and Wordiness

Responses will vary, but one possible revision is provided here.

Telling time is of great importance to us all, even though the concept of time has changed. Time is important in people's lives because it is the essential measure against which other important measurements are made. For example, we measure our bodies' heart rates and how fast our cars travel in terms of time. We organize our days and nights into segments of time, and from the beginnings of civilization people have counted the passage of time by counting sunrises and sunsets or the movements of the moon and the sun. For centuries, speculation about the nature of time was mostly a philosophical discussion of how people perceive time and experience its passage. But in twentieth-century science, since Albert Einstein, physicists have come to realize that time is a dimension of the physical universe. Time is a measure of motion in space, not some philosophical or theoretical thing that exists in people's minds. Einstein also showed that time is not absolute or unique. People used to think that any event measured in time would be seen to take the same amount of time. That is, two clocks in accurate working order would agree on the time interval between two events. But the discovery that the speed of light appeared the same to every observer, no matter how he or she was moving, led to the theory of relativity. Now time is seen to be relative to the observer who measures it. Each observer can have his or her measure of time as recorded by the clock he or she carries. Clocks carried by different observers do not necessarily have to agree. This is a very different view of time from the older one that time is absolute. However, even with this notion that time is not absolute, we still use time as a means of measurement.

Chapter 34 Passive Voice Versus Active Voice

One possible rewrite of the paragraph is as follows:

European astronomers recently announced that they have discovered a new planet in our galaxy. They have given the planet -- technically an "exoplanet," because it exists outside of our solar system -- the rather dull name of "Gliese 581c," since it orbits the star Gliese 581. Gliese 581c has some unique characteristics that separate it from the other 220 exoplanets that astronomers have discovered so far. For instance, the European team believes that Gliese 581c has a substantial atmosphere and is likely to have oceans: two things that astrobiologists deem essential for life to evolve. Furthermore, the planet exists in the so-called "Goldilocks Zone," which means its orbit relative to its sun is ideal for supporting life. Best of all, it is not so far away that it would be impossible for us to travel there someday: it is only 20.5 light years away, which, in astronomical terms, is not very far at all.

Chapter 35 Unnecessary and Inappropriate Language

35c. Pretentious Language

2. Responses will vary, but one possible revision is provided here.

As the twenty-first century progresses, American colleges and universities are trying to appeal to diverse students and provide wider access by offering classes in various formats. Students may study in traditional classrooms or complete an entire degree online without ever coming to a campus. Online classes are conducted exclusively through the Internet. If you're considering online education, you should be aware of the personal characteristics necessary for success in this environment. You must be self-disciplined and not inclined to procrastinate, and you must have excellent reading skills. Contrary to what many students think, online classes are not easier, but require much more time and concentrated effort than traditional classes. If you earn a degree online, however, you will have excellent computer skills, as well as knowledge of the subject matter.

Chapter 36 Appropriate Language

36b. Levels of Formality

Responses will vary, but one possible revision is provided here.

Parents concerned about their infants being kidnapped have a new method for identifying the baby. In the past, parents have photographed the child or taken a set of fingerprints to store in computer banks. But these methods are not foolproof. Photographs can be deceiving, especially as children grow up, and fingerprints can be difficult to match. Now scientists concerned about the lack of methods to positively identify a baby have found a promising new approach. Couples can take a sample of their child's DNA material, which contains a large amount of genetic information unique to that child. A repository for storing this information has been set up in New Jersey. The files in this storage facility are then available for matching a sample to a strand of hair, a piece of skin, or a few drops of blood. This DNA "fingerprinting" can positively identify a child at any time in his or her life. The samples in storage can last for the individual's lifetime and many years beyond. Some adults, such as those in high-risk or dangerous occupations, have also become interested in being put on file.

36c. Emphasis

Parallelism: Answers will vary, of course, but here is one example of an acceptable (if grandiose) sentence:

Beauty is not the color of one's eyes, nor the shape of one's nose, nor the cut of one's chin, nor the number of teeth in one's head: it is, instead, the goodness and truth and charity and modesty and human warmth that exude from the spirit and lend strength and light to the world.

Striking Language: Answers will definitely vary! Most importantly, however, don't be afraid to experiment with combinations, even if the idea sounds weird at first. Example: "Wisdom is like coffee: you have to know when to stop adding cream and sugar."

36d. Denotation and Connotation

Responses will vary, but possible responses are provided here.

a.	famous		f.	used
b.	pushy		g.	soil
c.	conservative		h.	smell
d.	compulsive		i.	cheap
e.	sanitary engineer		j.	lavish

Chapter 37 Nonsexist Language

Responses will vary, but one possible revision is provided here.

In many suburban housing developments built during recent decades there are homeowners associations that enforce housing codes on all the homeowners. The average owners in such a suburb may think that they are free to paint their houses whatever color they like or park any kind of car in their driveways, but that is not the case. Homeowners associations often have a lawyer who spends his or her days enforcing the laws enacted by these associations. The laws see to it that all the members abide by the group's standards of good taste. No plastic flamingos are allowed on the lawn, and all house painters who work in the suburb know that they cannot use certain colors for house trim, such as bright pink or a gaudy yellow, because they have to follow community guidelines. When houses are built in new developments, there are usually restrictive covenants that force buyers to join the association, whether they like it or not. Even when people challenge the laws, they usually lose as the covenants are legally binding. It all starts with the builder because when builders build, they want to make certain that the land value for the community stays high so that they can continue to sell their houses at a good price. The builder often starts off as the chairperson of the homeowners association so that he or she can guide the formation of the rules and regulations. In one wealthy Florida community there are even regulations for local government and civil servants, including dress codes for police officers, taxi drivers, and mail carriers. The only challenges that have gotten through the courts are those that show some regulation discriminates on the basis of race, religion, sex, or other characteristics of the homeowner.

PART SEVEN
PUNCTUATION

Chapter 38 Commas

38a. Commas in Compound Sentences

In 1977 the flight of the little airplane, the Gossamer Condor, did not look very impressive, but it was indeed an historic flight. With wings of foam, balsa wood, and Mylar, the plane designed by Paul MacCready floated slowly and gracefully over the San Joaquin Valley and covered a mile or so in about eight minutes. What made it so historic was that the pilot was pedaling. The Gossamer Condor was only the first of MacCready's pedal-powered planes, and two years later the plane's successor, the Gossamer Albatross, crossed the English Channel. Some people say that MacCready is really the brains behind these inventions, but others feel that he receives undue credit for the work that others on the development teams do. However, MacCready was the first to use his observations of how birds fly, so his supporters feel that he is the genius who made human-powered flight possible. Other inventors were taking the conventional approach of trying to reduce drag as much as possible because they thought this approach would be the answer. The approaches of other inventors were to streamline their aircraft, or they tried to incorporate ways to increase the horsepower. Only MacCready applied the principle of vastly increasing the wing area and used materials to keep the overall weight down. The result was an aircraft that needed only the power output of a good bicyclist, and the Gossamer Condor now has a place of honor next to the *Spirit of St. Louis* in the Smithsonian Institute's National Air and Space Museum.

38b. Commas After Introductory Words, Phrases, and Clauses

Having won prizes with his first human-powered plane, Paul MacCready went on to build a faster and more powerful pedal-powered plane, the Gossamer Albatross. In less than two years after his first success, MacCready's second pedal-powered plane departed from Folkestone, England, in June, 1979, bound for France. Expecting the flight to take about two hours, MacCready allotted just enough water for the pilot to drink. The flight team who prepared the plane and assisted the pilot on the ground waited several weeks for the kind of calm weather that was needed. Consequently, the pilot took off, expecting to reach France before his endurance and the water gave out. But a head wind blew up soon after the pilot was aloft. An hour and a half later, he was only two-thirds of the way to France, and his legs were cramping from all the pedaling. Because everyone was sure they had to give up the attempt, the flight team was ready to hook a towline to the craft that would haul it ashore. Tired and about to give up, the pilot knew he had to gain altitude to get hooked to the towline. As he climbed, he found less wind and was able to press on. Almost three hours later, the pilot touched down at Cape Gris-Nez, in France, a minute short of his theoretical exhaustion point. The Gossamer Albatross had crossed the English Channel, powered only by the pilot.

38c. Commas with Essential and Nonessential Words, Phrases, and Clauses

After designing human-powered planes, Paul MacCready, a prize-winning inventor, went on to design a solar-powered plane. MacCready, however, realized that solar cells as an energy source for planes do not make any practical sense. But MacCready, who had long sympathized with environmental concerns, hoped to demonstrate that solar power has an important part in the world's energy future. Those who see solar energy as merely a minor source of energy for the future downplay the importance of such demonstrations. Others think solar power has simply not been adequately developed for practical use. The solar-powered plane that MacCready designed flew from Paris to the coast of England in 1981, cruising at 441 mph at an altitude of 11,000 feet. The plane, called the Solar Challenger, provided the stepping stone to MacCready's next flying machine, the Sunraycer, a solar-powered car.

38d-h. Commas in Series and Lists; Commas with Adjectives; Commas with Dates, Addresses, Geographical Names, and Numbers; Other Uses for Commas; Unnecessary Commas

The Sunraycer, which is a solar-powered lightweight car, was built to compete in the 1987 Race Across Australia. Designed by Paul MacCready, the car won the race from Darwin to Adelaide_ and is now in the Smithsonian Institute's National Museum of American History. With a total weight of 365 pounds, the car has a power output of about 1.8 horsepower at noon on a bright day, and it gets the electric power equivalent of 500 miles to the gallon. The Sunraycer, which presently holds the solar-powered speed record of 48.7 mph, averaged a little over 40 mph for much of the race. The car is so light_that when it made turns during testing, it often seemed in danger of blowing over. The engineers who worked on the Sunraycer_ended up putting two little ears on the top. "We're not sure why they work," said one engineer, "though they seem to help." In some ways the Sunraycer is not a prototype of electric cars for commercial use_ because the Sunraycer has bicycle-thin wheels, a driver's seat that requires the driver to lie flat, and very weak acceleration. However, many of Sunraycer's features were carried over into the electric car developed by General Motors. Like the Sunraycer, the GM car uses alternating current_ and can, therefore, get better performance. If electric-powered cars become widely popular in the future, Paul MacCready will feel that he had some small part in saving the environment.

38a-h Review of Comma Usage

1.	address	6.	introductory element
2.	no commas	7.	introductory element, date
3.	appositive	8.	no commas
4.	items in series	9.	compound sentence
5.	nonessential clause	10.	interrupter, contrasting element

Chapter 39 Apostrophes

In the game of baseball, batting slumps are one of a player's worst nightmares. When they are doing well, players attribute their successes to mysterious minor occurrences around them that then become habits_ the players keep up. After a game in which one baseball player who was wearing an old helmet with its side dented hit two triples, a home run, and a single, the player continued to wear that helmet for the rest of the season. Warding off evil spirits through superstitions is another thing baseball players do. One player always wears the green T-shirt from his_ university under his team's jersey. Another won't wear a jersey with any 6's in his player's number. Batting coaches spend hours watching videotapes with slumping players, trying to find what's causing the problem. They examine the player's batting stance or swing, but this does n't always provide useful clues. Some slumps happen when batters begin to worry too much about their misses and about everyone else's successes. But one coach thinks otherwise. He notes that some players_ start making adjustments when they've hit a double and want to hit farther or when a certain unusual pitch connected well with their bats. Players in their 30's complain of a different kind of slump. One bad day, says one over-30 player, may mean he is losing it, that his age has begun to take its toll. A hitter who is hot, on the other hand, tends to get possessive about a special bat and uses it until it breaks or its_ cracks begin to show. When that bat goes, the player sometimes loses confidence until he connects with a new bat that brings him a few homeruns_. A batter's life is_n't as easy as some people think it is.

Chapter 40 Semicolons

Junk mail used to be confined to print on paper; now it is appearing in people's mailboxes on videocassettes. Companies in the direct-mail business are now marketing inexpensive cardboard videocassettes that can carry a variety of messages, such as audiovisual advertisements, promotional premiums, and educational or training aids. Some companies are switching to this form of direct-mail advertising because it is relatively cheap; in addition, it presents messages more vividly on television screens than print advertising can on paper. Informational videos can be sent to prospective customers, and advertisers can use their product in the video. Says the spokesperson for one cereal company, "We are interested in promoting good nutritional habits"; as might be expected, the balanced diet they will be picturing in the video will include their cereal. Printed instructions in merchandise are often confusing; consequently, some manufacturers are also switching to these disposable videocassettes for the instructional packets they include with their merchandise. The cardboard videocassettes are relatively cheap to manufacture and cheap to mail. They are certainly more convenient than the promotional packets sent by companies that have relied on enclosing sample packets of toothpaste, aspirin, or cereal; mail advertisers who send bulky envelopes of coupons; and companies who want to entice customers with big brochures of vacation places, hotels, and tours. The disposable videocassette is certainly going to grow in popularity as an advertising medium.

Chapter 41 Colons

Evaluating college teachers is a complex, often difficult task. Now a new method devised in the Midwest is being tried out across the nation: the teaching portfolio. Administrators and faculty members see the portfolio, a collection of materials documenting classroom performance, as a way to emphasize teaching as a major priority. Too often, professors who are being evaluated document primarily their research and scholarly activities, such as published books and articles, lists of grants, and conference presentations. Says one faculty member at a large Eastern university: "When it comes to teaching, most teachers only have student evaluations and coffee-room conversations about what they do in class and how their students are learning"; this kind of evidence is not very thorough or sufficient to determine pay raises, tenure, and promotion. As a result, many faculty members are judged and rewarded on the basis of their research and publications. Their teaching performance, whether outstanding or mediocre, is largely ignored. The portfolio can be a better measure of what faculty really do as teachers, for the portfolio can consist of the following items: a statement of the person's teaching philosophy, a list of the courses that person has taught, a representative syllabus, statements by fellow faculty members who have observed this person, and course materials that the person has prepared. At some schools where portfolios are already in use, the portfolios also include unsolicited letters from former students, teaching awards, and even videotapes of the candidate teaching a class. Some faculty members who have prepared these portfolios say that there is an added advantage: the portfolio collection can lead to self-improvement. This can happen when the process of creating the collection causes the person to think seriously about teaching goals, strategies, and results.

Chapter 42 Quotation Marks

"Why am I fatter than my sister-in-law? I eat less," complained a woman being studied by a team of researchers. She explained that she repeatedly went on diets when her sister-in-law didn't. But the woman continues to weigh more. Researchers are finding out that heredity, in addition to lifestyle, exerts a strong influence on people's weight. By studying identical and fraternal twins, research teams are finding that brothers and sisters end up with similar body weights whether or not they are raised in different families. In the *Journal of Genetics*, Dr. Albert Skinnerd writes, "When the biological parents are fat, there is an 80 percent chance that their children will also be overweight" (234). "Does this mean that my brother and I are doomed to be fat?" asked one overweight twin in the study. Since some sets of twins tend to transform extra calories into fat while other sets of twins tend to convert extra calories into muscle, one scientist concluded that "genes do seem to have something to do with the amount you gain when you overeat." Some unsuccessful dieters may be relieved to know that their failed diets aren't a matter of failed willpower. "It is really a matter of metabolism," reports another doctor doing research in this field. But that does not mean that low-fat diets and exercise should be given up. "'Quit' is not a word in my vocabulary," says one constant dieter who manages to maintain a reasonable weight by means of careful eating and plenty of exercise, despite a tendency to be overweight.

Chapters 43, 44, 45 Hyphens, End Punctuation, and Other Punctuation

1.   Which oils are good for us to eat? A study of thirty-nine participants on a reduced-fat diet looked at the benefits of consuming olive oil and/or corn oil. Which is more beneficial in influencing high-density lipoprotein levels—corn oil or olive oil? This is an important question because high-density lipoprotein (HDL) is considered a beneficial form of cholesterol that helps remove the more dangerous low-density lipoproteins from the body. In a study published in an article, "Two Healthy Oils for Human Consumption" (*Diet and Health News* 14 [1991]: 22-36), researchers report that the participants first spent twelve weeks on a diet that included olive oil and then another twelve weeks on a corn-oil diet. The results (which were also announced on television newscasts) indicated that neither diet resulted in lower levels of HDL. This indicates that a diet of olive oil and/or corn oil can accompany a reduced-fat diet. For those who self-select the oils they use in their diet, the choice is probably a matter of taste or cost.

2.   Do you see that green area to the left of the river we are flying over?" said the pilot to the passengers as the commercial 747 jet flew over southern Texas. Continued the pilot, "That's my grandfather's ranch. I often visited there as a kid." Public address systems in commercial planes are now being used by pilots to enliven their passengers' flights. Some pilots are opposed to this practice because they see it as a distraction. Says one seasoned veteran, "Our task... is to fly the plane, not amuse the passengers." But others disagree. Interesting, informative comments can put nervous passengers more at ease and can shorten a long flight. For those pilots interested in making such public-address announcements, there is now a book put together by an ex-pilot which pinpoints more than 1,200 historical and little-known places of interest on a collection of highway maps of the U.S. The maps are overlaid with the flight paths used by commercial pilots. Are you flying between El Paso, Texas, and Las Vegas, New Mexico? If so, then look for the site of the Berringer Crater, where a meteor hit with such force 22,000 years ago that it killed all animal and plant life within 100 miles! Thousands of these maps have been sold, with more frequent fliers than pilots doing the buying. "We are learning...an awful lot about territory we thought we knew!" says one frequent flier who takes her book with her on every flight. Another customer reports, "I bought one for my uncle who hates airplanes, and he now actually enjoys his flights." The book is obviously a success. Is the author correct when he says, "Soon, there will be such books in the pocket of every seat in every commercial flight"?

PART EIGHT
MECHANICS AND SPELLING

Chapters 46, 47, 48 Capitals, Abbreviations, and Numbers

One of Boston's most popular folk heroes is Paul Revere, whose midnight ride was made famous in Longfellow's poem, "Paul Revere's Ride," in *Tales of a Wayside Inn*. Not many tourists realize that many of the places mentioned in that poem are still part of Boston's twentieth-century landscape, along what is commonly called the Freedom Trail. This well-marked trail is actually a two-mile line in red paint, bricks, or steps with twenty-one historic buildings, sites, and monuments documenting Boston's contribution to American history. Two miles isn't long, but it usually takes tourists who are thorough two or three days to see everything on the trail. Most begin at the Boston Common, the oldest public park in the United States. Here colonists used the public land for grazing animals, training the militia, and staging public executions. Immediately next to the Common is America's first public botanical garden, the Boston Public Garden, famous partly because it was the setting for the well-known children's book, *Make Way for Ducklings*. Just across the street, on Beacon Street, is another of Boston's famous sites, the Old State House, completed in 1798. Its cornerstone was laid by Samuel Adams in 1793. One block east on Beacon Street and then one block south on Park Street is the historic Park Street Church on the corner of Tremont. Here the song "America" was first sung on July 4, 1831. The next stop on the Freedom Trail is the Granary Burying Ground, a cemetery on Tremont Street. Some of the greatest U.S. patriots, including Paul Revere, Samuel Adams, John Hancock, James Otis, etc., are buried here. Also along Tremont Street, at the corner of School Street, is King's Chapel, the first Anglican church in Boston. After the revolution, it became the first Unitarian church in the country, and its cemetery contains the graves of many other early notables, including William Dawes, Jr., and Gov. John Winthrop. (It was Governor Winthrop who headed the group that founded the Boston colony.) Also on School Street is the first public school in America, which later became the Boston Public Latin School. Rev. Cotton Mather, Ralph Waldo Emerson, John Hancock, Benjamin Franklin, et al., were alumni of this school. These are only a few of the many sights along the Freedom Trail. Longfellow's poem says, "Hardly a man is now alive who remembers that famous day and year...." True, but the Freedom Trail helps visitors realize many of the events that led to our nation's independence.

Chapter 49 Underlining/Italics

a.	U	k.	U
b.	U	l.	Q
c.	Q	m.	U
d.	U	n.	Q
e.	U	o.	U
f.	Q	p.	U
g.	Q	q.	U
h.	U	r.	U
i.	U	s.	Q
j.	Q	t.	U

Chapter 50 Spelling

50a. Proofreading

Inventors of gadgets for automobiles <u>haven't</u> always been successful with <u>their</u> inventions. But we can see from some <u>of</u> these inventions that people have been looking for ways to make cars more <u>functional</u>, better looking, and more fun to drive. <u>For</u> example, we now have <u>elegant</u> and sophisticated ways to <u>hear</u> music in <u>our</u> cars, but some of the earlier ways to add music to driving seem a bit odd now. In the <u>1920s</u>, Daniel Young <u>received</u> a patent for an organ he invented for use in automobiles. He built organ keyboards that could be attached to <u>the</u> back of the front seat so that people <u>riding</u> in the back could play the organ to entertain <u>themselves</u>. This may have been a good idea, <u>except</u> for one thing. The roads of that time, <u>unfortunately</u>, were so bumpy and uneven that the sounds <u>produced</u> by the organ when the car was moving <u>were anything</u> but beautiful. Another <u>terrific</u> idea that didn't make it was Leander Pelton's patent for a car that could be parked by standing it on end. Instead of a back <u>bumper</u>, he built a vertical platform with <u>rollers</u> attached. When parking the Vertical Park Car, the driver needed to tip the car back onto <u>the</u> platform. <u>Then</u> he could just shove the car into any <u>appropriately</u> sized space. To <u>perform</u> this task, however, was a <u>bit difficult</u> as Pelton never quite explained how the car was to be <u>tipped</u> from <u>horizontal</u> to vertical and back down again. A <u>different</u> problem was that Pelton didn't <u>provide</u> any way to keep gasoline, water, and oil from spilling once the car was up on its <u>parking</u> rollers. But the <u>government</u> gave him a patent; he simply couldn't get anyone to <u>manufacture</u> his Vertical-Park <u>Car</u>. Another invention that never made it was designed by Joseph Grant in 1926—an <u>automobile washing</u> machine. The <u>machine</u> didn't wash cars, but it <u>supposedly</u> washed clothes. Grant's invention <u>consisted</u> of a tub and paddles that bolted to the car's <u>running</u> boards. <u>When</u> the tub was filled with water, soap, and <u>dirty</u> clothes, the bouncing of the car over <u>rough</u> roads provided all the power and <u>agitation</u> necessary to clean a load of dirty clothes. For <u>really</u> dirty <u>loads</u>, an extra twenty miles or so of driving was <u>recommended</u>.

50c. Some Spelling Guidelines

1. IE/EI

a. believe	f. weird	k. neither
b. yield	g. field	l. ceiling
c. seize	h. eight	m. niece
d. height	i. deceive	n. neighbor
e. foreign	j. financier	o. vein

2. Doubling Consonants

a. napping	e. writing	i. beginning
b. footing	f. referred	j. benefited
c. starred	g. hopped	k. shopping
d. tapping	h. occurrence	l. omitted

50e. Sound-Alike Words (Homonyms)

a. except

b. accept

c. affected

d. effect

e. here

f. It's

g. it's

h. its

i. passed

j. than

k. then

l. then

m. there, their

n. to, too

o. were

p. who's

q. you're, your

r. advice, buying

s. site

t. quite

u. stationary

v. already

w. all right

x. any one

y. all together

PART NINE
ESL AND MULTILINGUAL WRITERS

Chapter 52 Verbs

1.   When people from other countries <u>shop</u> in American supermarkets, they find an amazing supply of items other than grocery items. On one aisle, a shopper <u>will discover</u>, for example, toiletry items such as toothbrushes, toothpaste, deodorant, and shampoo. On another aisle <u>are</u> paper towels, garbage bags, and cleaning supplies. Sometimes the choices <u>are</u> confusing. But the choices <u>do not end</u> with the shopping itself. Even when the shopping <u>has concluded</u>, the shopper may have decisions to make. For example, the person behind the checkout counter <u>may ask</u> if the customer <u>wants</u> the purchases in a plastic bag. Of course, if Americans <u>were</u> to shop in stores and bazaars in other countries, they <u>would</u> find the process just as confusing.

2.   In the United States, students hope <u>to learn</u> more than just the subject matter they are studying. They believe that if they <u>study</u> a subject thoroughly, ask questions, and even <u>disagree</u> with certain opinions of writers and scholars, they <u>will become</u> better thinkers as well. Students from other countries may find it difficult at first to practice critical thinking skills in American classrooms because <u>questioning</u> an authority or the written word may be a sign of disrespect in their country. Another problem that students from other countries may encounter in American classrooms involves writing assignments. Whereas American students are comfortable with <u>choosing</u> topics for writing that argue accepted ideas, students from other countries may have difficulty <u>expressing</u> their opinions without <u>apologizing</u> for them because <u>discussing</u> controversial topics may be considered rude in their country. Obviously, students' cultural backgrounds affect many aspects of college life, including how they approach the educational experience.

Chapter 53 Omitted Words

When importing ivory became illegal in the United States in 1989, engineers and material scientists searched for substitutes for natural ivory. For piano makers, the ban on ivory brought on the problem of how to make piano keys after the supply on hand <u>was</u> used up. While conservationists and elephant lovers want people <u>to</u> stop using ivory, many pianists who have tested plastic substitutes <u>are</u> about to abandon hope of having new pianos with satisfactory substitutes. However, <u>there</u> may be a solution. A team of experts has produced a substitute that may satisfy many piano builders and piano players. This new synthetic ivory both resembles natural ivory and has a similar microscopic structure. But even with a substitute for piano keys now available, the market for ivory <u>may</u> not decrease as piano makers <u>have</u> never been major consumers of ivory. The largest consumers of ivory in the world are Asian manufacturers of signature stamps, but even <u>they</u> have given up their use of ivory and <u>are</u> switching to substitutes.

Chapter 54 Repeated Words

a.   Students in my class <u>they</u> are looking forward to the upcoming vacation.
b.   The book that 1 wanted to read <u>it</u> was not in the library.
c.   My teacher found the book that I left <u>it</u> in the classroom.
d.   The apartment building where I live <u>there</u> has two swimming pools.
e.   The child returned the dog that I had lost <u>it</u>.
f.   The pie in the refrigerator <u>it</u> is for tonight's party.
g.   The book drop where library books are placed <u>there</u> is full.
h.   My aunt called on the new cellular telephone that she had <u>it</u> installed in her car.

Chapter 55 Count and Noncount Nouns

In American supermarkets, new <u>products</u> and <u>produce</u> are constantly being added to the shelves. Children are attracted to new snack foods, and adults are frequently tempted to buy items with <u>information</u> about health benefits. To increase consumer <u>confidence</u> in package labeling, the Food and Drug Administration has announced new <u>guidelines</u> for various claims food manufacturers add to their labels. Products that are advertised as "low fat" have to provide <u>evidence</u> on the label and meet new government <u>standards</u>. For items that appeal to children, the amount of <u>sugar</u> must be clearly indicated. Particularly helpful are the new regulations on serving size because consumers in America have become very conscious of the amount of <u>protein</u> and <u>fat</u> that they eat as well as the number of <u>calories</u>.

Chapter 56 Adjectives and Adverbs

56c-d. A/An/The, Some/Any, Much/Many, Little/Few, Less/Fewer, Enough, No

In northern India there is <u>a</u> conflict between wildlife officials and Gujjar herders of water buffalo. <u>The</u> Indian Government wants to turn the area into a national park, to be called the Fajaji National Park, but for the last ten years, local water buffalo herders refuse to move off the land. The Gujjars keep herding their water buffalo, despite warnings that the animals are eating up too <u>much</u> of the vegetation and that soon there will be <u>few</u> areas that have not been destroyed by the herding. Several decades ago, the Gujjars agreed to migrate every summer to give the forests a chance to grow again, but communities in the areas they migrated to refused to accept the Gujjars because they needed <u>the</u> land for their own grazing, and they didn't have <u>enough</u> land to share. As a result, the Gujjars now stay in the forest throughout <u>the</u> year. Government officials keep on warning of <u>the</u> dangers of erosion in the forests where Gujjar herding has stripped the land. While <u>some</u> environmental groups say that these forest dwellers have as much right to the land as the animals, other groups support the government's attempt to move the Gujjars. The continued grazing by water buffalo risks using up the <u>few</u> food sources of elephants and other animals. Government officials plan to make <u>an</u> offer to the Gujjars to move them to settlements on the edge of the forests and to have them feed their animals in stalls. Park officials want to find <u>a</u> solution soon because they say that both the park and the Gujjars will suffer if the present situation continues.

Chapter 57
Prepositions

1.   Birmingham <u>in</u> the spring of 1923 was a comparatively new and modern city. Lacking the Old South cultural heritage <u>of</u> the older southern cities such as Atlanta or Nashville, it was characterized <u>by</u> a tremendous energy and pursuit <u>of</u> success that one would expect <u>in</u> an emerging industrial giant. As such, it was somewhat <u>of</u> a melting pot <u>with</u> a constantly increasing number of new residents. Many were <u>from</u> the rural areas of the South, both black and white. There were also significant numbers of immigrants <u>from</u> Italy, Ireland, Germany, and the eastern European countries impoverished <u>by</u> war and other social and political factors. There also were smaller numbers <u>of</u> Asians and others. Inevitably, competition and distrust existed <u>between</u> these various groups, but gradually these were worked out <u>in</u> most cases.

PART TEN
RESEARCH

Chapter 59 Finding A Topic

59a. Deciding on a Purpose and Audience

1. Below are several non-exclusive ways to begin determining which movies you might use for the paper. The list is by no means exhaustive.

    A.   Review your class notes, searching for insights from your professor and other classmates as to which movies were most important.

    B.   Directly ask your professor for suggestions; also, ask professors you know from other classes, as well as a librarian.

    C.   Ask family members and friends for their input.

    D.   Go to the library and search film and media databases, looking for books and papers that have analyzed Vietnam War films.

    E.   Use your favorite search engine to look for movie web sites and blogs that discuss Vietnam War movies.

    F.   After doing some or all of the above, watch some of the suggested movies (or, if you have seen them before, watch them again), and take notes.

2. To "prove" what each movie's message is, so that you can compare their similarities and differences, you might, among other things:

    A.   Write down what you thought of each film the first time you watched it. Value your own first impression!

    B.   Take careful notes as you watch each film, noting important elements of the plot, the characters, the setting, the style of direction, any symbols and motifs that recur in the film, etc.

    C.   Check out a few books from the library on how to analyze films. Again, ask your librarian for suggestions.

    D.   Read what other people have said about these films in books, academic journals, popular magazines, newspapers and blogs. Note: for a research paper, you will likely need to use academic sources such as books and journal articles more than popular magazines, newspapers and blogs. At this early stage, however, popular sources can help you formulate your own ideas.

3. Since this paper's audience is a "generally well-educated American audience," you will need to include explanations of any names, dates, locations, cultural references, military tactics, geographical conditions, and other information that is specific to the Vietnam War. A good measure for what to include in your explanations is this question: "Did I learn this piece of information in class, or did I know it beforehand?" If you knew the piece of information in question before you started the course, it is likely a piece of general knowledge (unless you are a history major!). Otherwise, it is probably specific enough to warrant explanation and exploration in your paper.

4. Since the goal of the paper is not to explore filmmaking techniques in and of themselves, but to demonstrate how these techniques fit in with the film's overall themes,
you should present only enough technical information to guarantee your audience understands how those techniques influence our understanding of the film. For instance, an analysis of Apocalypse Now might delve into how Coppola's desire to create a special theater to show the film, complete with vibrating seats, demonstrates his desire to create not so much a "movie" as an "event"; on the other hand, enumerating which specific machines he used to edit the film might prove superfluous (or might not, depending on the context).

5. On the surface, the assignment may seem to indicate that the professor is more interested in a viewpoint-neutral research paper than in seeing a thesis-driven one. Note, however, that the assignment asks students to choose the

three movies that they believe are "most representative of the genre." Furthermore, students must discuss the similarities and differences between movies; this part of the assignment is also subjective, as it calls for deductions and opinions on the students' part. With these factors in mind, students should understand that, while they will be conducting a research-based analysis in this paper, that analysis must be framed in terms of their own point of view: a thesis.

Always ask your professors to clarify any part of a research paper assignment that is not clear to you!

Chapter 60 Searching for Information

60a. Choosing Primary and Secondary Sources

1. secondary
2. primary
3. secondary

4. secondary
5. primary
6. secondary

PART ELEVEN
MLA DOCUMENTATION

PART TWELVE
APA, CM, AND CSE DOCUMENTATION

Chapter 68 Documenting in Other Styles

1. C

2. E

3. A

4. B

5. D